Pages
C

John Hercus

solway

Copyright © John Hercus 1996

First published 1962 by Inter-Varsity Press,
38 de Montfort Street, Leicester, LE1 7GP

Second Edition 1964
Reprinted 1965, 1967, 1969, 1972

This edition 1996 by Solway

02 01 00 99 98 97 96   7 6 5 4 3 2 1

Solway is an imprint of Paternoster Publishing,
P.O. Box 300, Carlisle, Cumbria CA3 0QS U.K.

British Library Cataloguing in Publication Data

A catalogue record for this book is available from the British Library.

ISBN 1–900507–05–6

Printed in the U.K. by Cox & Wyman Ltd., Reading

CONTENTS

CHAPTER ONE

THE CASES ARE SELECTED

I N the early 'twenties my dad acquired a T-Model 'Ford'. Most of it had left the assembly line in 1914, but all of it needed regular treatment. I well remember one such treatment day. My father and an uncle were 'testing the plugs'. The old Lizzies had four cylinders, but they oiled-up badly, especially number one, and regular cleaning of oiled plugs was simply part of the joyous story of motoring. But they were always 'tested' first, just on the off-chance that number one was innocent, and two, three or four was really the culprit.

You know the technique? Short-circuit each plug in turn by means of a screwdriver held to the cylinder block. Then the faulty plug is found easily enough, because either you don't get big fat sparks from it, or the uneven engine beat isn't changed. This was the first time I had ever seen it done. It was the first time I had ever seen electricity in close action. I was goggle-eyed at the miniature lightning my dad was producing We still had no electricity in our town, but this was certainly electricity. I quietly and quickly picked up the screwdriver and put it on the nearest plug. I shall never forget the stunned amazement with which the car and the garage and the floor and my uncle (who had his hand on my arm, it seems) and about a hundred invisible prizefighters all hit me at once! The trouble was that nobody had told me anything about holding the screwdriver by the handle! I began to learn about electricity.

And then the power did come to our town. We had electric lights. And an electric stove. And an electric hot-water system. The first electric stove *and* hot-water system in the whole town. My elder brother (and I) learned All-About-It. When we developed a short-circuit in the stove one day, We Knew. We put in a

thicker fuse-wire. When that blew out, We Still Knew.
We doubled it. Then re-doubled it. Then re-re-doubled
it. Then put in a stout sixteen-gauge copper wire. That
didn't blow. That held splendidly, as with an exciting
flash the Supply Authority's fuses blew out in the road,
and Selkirk Street was plunged into blackness. We
hastily removed our piece of copper wire, put in a
single strand of fuse-wire, and rang the electrician.
No doubt some benighted neighbour rang the Supply
Authority, because in due time a lorry arrived with
men and ladders, and the lights came on again. We
were learning more electricity!

And then my elder brother (the journeyman) and I
(the apprentice) made a little electric motor. I can still
remember vividly every detail of that little affair. Its
three-pole laminated armature, its crude but effective
commutator, the brushes made from rolled-up fine-
mesh brass gauze, and the field magnet—all wound
with 26-gauge enamelled copper wire. We learned to
wind it in series; we learned to wind it in shunt.

One day we mounted this little motor in a Meccano
cage, and set it on two pieces of light galvanized iron
fencing wire strung tightly across the kitchen about
two feet from the floor. We then connected these two
wires to the 240-volt house current in series with the
toaster and, taking a lead to the little motor in the
cage, we had surely the prettiest miniature mountain
railway that ever you saw! Backwards and forwards,
with our reversing switch, we had it running across
the kitchen, sparks flying from the overhead wires, a
veritable shower of sparks blazing around the commutator. And with it all the pungent smell of burning
oil from the brushes. We thought this was Ozone, and
very health-promoting! Our little sister, who was just
a toddler, was watching from a distance of about twelve
inches, simply enchanted.

And then Mother came home—and was terrified.
'You'll kill yourselves!' she exclaimed. 'And the baby!'

'No, Mum!' we said, patronizingly.'It's perfectly safe.'

'But the electrician said the electricity in the powerpoint was as much as a kick from seven horses!' (I know he said that; I heard him. I have never known what he meant, unless it was that he had it wired for twenty amps.)

'Look, Mum. It's as safe as a bank. We have it going through the toaster, and that chews up all the juice. This little motor only takes a few volts.' We knew all-about-electricity!

How very fortunate it is that mothers have the power of veto! I, and my brother, and our little sister, are all still alive!

And then, to crown all, we exchanged the old 'Ford' for a 1925 model, brand new, with electric lights, electric horn, and, wonder of wonders, an electric self-starter. Electricity was now bread-and-butter stuff.

You may imagine then, perhaps, how my feelings were when I began to study matriculation electricity at school. Our master took us through carefully-defined concepts of electrostatic charge, potential, potential difference, capacity, current. I was longing for news of motors and buzzers and lamps, and perhaps even radio —I did so very much want a crystal set. But we went on to Oersted and his discovery of electro-magnetism, and Ohm and his law with the new concept of resistance. This world was only theory; my other earlier world only practice. The theory was objective, detached, an abstraction. The practice had been hit-and-miss, experimental, backyard stuff.

And then the master broke the barrier, by a simple teaching trick. He gave us a little picture talk, an illustration from another part of life, to make us understand the cold theory. It ran like this:

Think of electricity as being like water flowing in pipes. The quantity of electricity (Coulombs to us) is like gallons of water. If the pressure is high, a good flow will result. If the pipes are narrow, they will conduct less water. The same with electricity. Pressure is volts, potential difference. The flow is amps, q per second. The narrow pipes are like narrow conductors —they have a high resistance (ohms) to flow.

It was very simple. Even I could follow it now. And as I thought back from the simple picture analogy, I found the earlier abstraction easy to understand. And finally I learned to think from the abstraction itself, and didn't need to refer to the water in pipes again.

Now that is one of the valuable teaching methods that all good teachers use over and over again. It is a matter of taking an illustration, a picture, from some well-known area of experience, and using it to teach some part of a new truth.

But note this carefully: if I had grown up in some primitive culture where I had never seen water flowing under pressure in pipes, the illustration itself would have been completely useless, and in using it the master would have been making confusion worse confounded!

Physics is a delightful clear-cut, straightforward subject. A good teacher can make any of the concepts in elementary Physics clear if he sets out to use his imagination and think out simple pictures, like this one our schoolmaster gave us in electricity. The abstractions are themselves clearly defined ('Learn your definitions and you know your Physics', we were taught) and simple picture illustrations can be found in almost every conceivable background of life.

But if this is simple in Physics, it is certainly not so in Theology. Theology is the knowledge of God; and God is Spirit. To dust-begotten creatures like ourselves He is unknowable. The only things we can ever know of Him are the things He Himself reveals to us. Thus the abstract truths concerning the Nature of God, concerning His will for us, concerning our right relationship to Him—these are truths we could never conceivably know unless God tells them to us.

We, as Christians, claim that these things, concerning His plan and purpose for us, have been revealed to us. And we hasten to stress that to have this knowledge is not an achievement on our part, and does not in itself imply any favourable relationship between ourselves and God.

Then where do we receive this information? How does God tell it to us? Is its source to be found in the quiet musings of a walk in the hills? Is it in the warm emotional pressure of a revival meeting? Is it in the sacraments?

No. Not in any of these, or anything like these. It may well be expressed in these ways, but it does not originate in them. The source of this all-important knowledge is in fact recorded in a book. Some learned men prefer to read this book in Elizabethan English, and I have met a very few, of extreme ability, who read it even in Greek and Hebrew, the languages in which much of it was originally written. But simple people like myself prefer to read it in our own ordinary language—and you may buy it from any bookseller for less than a guinea, in good print and well bound.

Suppose then that you have paid out your guinea and have been reading your Bible in modern English. You will have noticed that a lot of it is anecdote and family history—some of it is in fact History in the bigger sense. It is embarrassingly free of Science, while it abounds in dreams and visions and miracles and portents. And it includes no less than four separate accounts of the story of God when He became man, and lived and died here on earth. These four records are most unimpressive in their reporting techniques, as compared with the *Daily Mirror* and the *Evening News*; but they are uniquely impressive in the impact made by the central Figure of the narrative. Then there is found a rather scrappy bit of record of the early Christian Church; a few letters from prominent Christian people; and finally a most exotic, trance-like vision in which we read an attempt made by a man to record something not just intended for human mind—no less a wonder than 'A revelation God gave to Jesus Christ'.

This book, then, is the means God has chosen to tell us what He wants from us, and in which He goes on to tell us what He plans to do to us (should I say 'to do *for* us'?) and even to hint how He will go about it.

In this book we read how this was taught in part to
a theologically 'primitive' man like Abraham; and how
it was taught much more fully to a much more 'ad-
vanced' man like Jeremiah; and how it is taught in the
fullest possible way to us.

Now God is the really expert Teacher. In fact He
is *the* Teacher. And He knows all the wise teaching
methods. He has recorded for us several accounts of
how He has taught men by the experimental methods
I first used when learning electricity. I can think immediately of one man who took a spiritual screwdriver
and plonked it on the nearest spark-plug. And got a
million-volt spark! But he was more venturesome than
ever I was—he tried it again! Another million volts!
Good old Gideon and his fleece. Aren't most of us little-
boy enough to hanker after the screwdriver and the
big sparks, the wet fleece and the dry fleece of the
Gideon story?

But there is not a great deal of that sort of story,
because that is the story of children, and God is always
wanting us to grow up. And it is dangerous; and over-
painful.

A great deal of the teaching is in fact done through
illustrations, through pictures—pictures of all kinds,
taken from all sorts of human experiences. Let me in-
dicate a few.

As you read your Bible, on one occasion you may
perhaps find that God is in fact using the picture of
'ransom', to teach His truth. It is a huge picture, drawn
on a national scale, a picture painted by the story of
His own people getting caught up as slaves in enemy
territory; and of His redeeming them back into freedom. See how often the New Testament writers draw
on this picture to tell us of Jesus, the Redeemer. Hear
from His own lips the statement: 'The Son of man
has come to give his life a ransom for many.'

Again, you are reading, and this time the picture is
all legal. Rules, ethics, laws, commands, which God
says we must keep. You have that sick feeling of seeing
an examination paper with all the tough, impossible

questions—not a single one you can begin to answer.
And as you read on, in this all-important examination
of the accused in the Court of Righteousness, you come
on something that takes your breath away. A man is
standing there, undergoing this tremendous trial, when
the Judge says: 'Stop this case. This man is completely
righteous. Everything he did was justified!'

And the Bible is full of this. It says this about Moses.
Fair enough, you say. Moses is the most sublime mind
in history. Moses today would rate at least as M.D.,
D.Sc., D.D., LL.D., D.Litt. Yes; but it also says exactly
the same about Noah, whose obscene drunkenness em-
barrasses us as much as it did his sons; and about
Lot, who was a low-down, incestuous old rotter if
ever there was one; and about Rahab, a prostitute;
and about Jacob; and about Jephthah; and about all
sorts of average people and decent people and complete no-hopers. (And even, dare I say, as I read,
about me?)

What a tremendous picture! No wonder St. Paul
used it so much, with his strong legal and Pharisaic
background. 'One hundred per cent!' the Judge has
been saying. High Distinction! First Class Honours.
University Medal. *Summa cum laude.* Change the language picture, and we hear the King saying, 'Yes, come
along in, you who have won My Father's blessing. Take
your inheritance—the kingdom reserved for you from
the foundation of the world.'

But as you read, as you are seeing this picture, you
hear the same Judge say to another man, 'Take him
out and beat him soundly. He is a wicked man.' A
miserable failure. No marks at all. Nought per cent.
And you can even find some of them arguing with the
Judge: 'But, Sir, I did mighty fine works in Your
Name.' 'And Sir, I expounded the truth in Your
Name.' And the Judge cuts them short, as He bursts
in: 'Quiet! I never even knew you. Go away from Me.
You are evil-doers, you are cursed.'

'And they will go away into eternal punishment, but
the righteous into eternal life.'

What a wonderful—and what a terrifying—court scene this is!

And you read again, and it's a very different picture. Now it's a book of saviours. A tale of people in a mess, and someone coming and pulling them out of the mess, and fixing their affairs comfortably and securely again. And hence one obvious way of depicting Him is to describe Him as the Saviour.

And next time it is all sacrifice. A particular sort of sacrifice, in which a man's guilt is ceremonially carried by an innocent beast. This is a picture found in many religions, but nowhere so clearly and consis tently as in the old Hebrew ritual. No wonder, then, that John, the baptizer, a Jew, announces Jesus as 'the Lamb of God'.

And so on. Illustration is piled on illustration, cen tury after century, page after page. Adoption, re-birth or re-generation, covenant, 'types', re-creation. (This last is the one I think I like best; it seems so easy to understand in our modern, manufacturing, Western world.) God seems to be willing to use a tremendous variety of pictures to make the central truth clear.

And that, today, seems to be a lot of the trouble Our reading is not careful enough to have the illustra tions clear, and our teachers and preachers often seem rather vague about them also. It is rather like teaching an Australian aboriginal the theory of electricity by means of the illustration of water flowing under pres sure in pipes when he has never seen water in pipes at all!

That is the difficulty today with many of these Bible pictures. For example, our saviours today are too im personal to teach us clearly the Bible meaning of the word 'saviour'. Our saviours now are radar, nuclear fission, antibiotics, insurance policies, pensions and the like. Oh yes, we had a Winston Churchill, and Lloyd George before him; and we have a lot of confidence in the very lovely young woman who is our Queen. But the picture is not at all a clear and simple one. Cer tainly it is nothing like as forceful as the experience of the Gileadites when Jephthah saved them from the Ammonites; or the experience of the tribes of Naphtali and Zebulun when Barak saved them from Sisera and his nine hundred chariots of iron.

Again the very important and much-drawn picture of sacrifice that so often dominates the Bible record has, so far as I know, no counterpart in our modern life whatsoever. So far is this removed from our culture that a lot of theologians even say that it just cannot be true—the very idea of one man taking another's guilt is simply immoral, and is a hideous carry-over into Christian literature of barbaric ideas from Hebrew and pre-Hebrew sources. You see, they have apparently failed to understand the facet of truth which this picture is teaching, and have thought of the picture as if it were the reality. So also with 'ransom' and 'redemption'. We are today so many centuries removed from any memory of personal slavery that the whole imagery is entirely theoretical.[1]

Yes, pictures are wonderful teaching aids—provided the class can understand the picture itself. But they can be confusing too.

When we were students, by the time we were in our fourth year we had some knowledge of some diseases, though we had never as yet seen actual cases. We had seen a Pneumococcus under the microscope; we had seen lung consolidated by the inflammatory reaction this toxic little enemy sets up; we had been told the (then) theory of antigens and antibodies; we had had it explained to us that if the blood could get through

[1] The unparalleled level of slavery into which the Western world has in fact sunk is not of course recognized by us as being bondage at all. Why, we ourselves forged the fetters! We are always shoving each other out of the way, in our eagerness to be more manacled! We think there is something wrong with a man when he declares that he is a bit bothered by it all. Our technologies, our professions, our elaborate Social Services— why, these are the great emancipating elements in Western culture, we say; these are the things that provide our Four Freedoms! Oh well; as a doctor I must admit that a lot of my income is in fact derived from the stress in which people are finding themselves, hampered by so much 'Freedom'.

one lung, but the air could not reach it, then the blood would return to the heart unoxygenated, and the patient would look blue. And so on, and so on, and so on.

Until we were at last taken into the wards, and the busy tutors would snatch an hour or so to teach us something. 'There,' the tutor would say as we would stop at the foot of a bed. 'Pneumonia. Here is the Path. report—Type II. Look at the temperature chart— sudden rise as the toxins are produced; falls suddenly on sixth day, as antibodies win through. Crisis—re- member the word? See that blue-looking man down there in the second bed? Cyanosis, from unoxygenated blood. Listen to his chest—right lung—all the signs of consolidation. Look at the sputum in the mug— characteristic. Blood full of polymorphs. Compare that with the hydatid in the lung you saw in the surgical ward—different picture altogether.' And then off we would go to see the congenital heart, who was also blue, but for such a different reason again.

This was an entirely new method of teaching, one where we were learning from the cases themselves. We were no longer learning pneumonia from test-tubes and microscopes and bottles, but from the thing itself, from the case of pneumonia.

Now in His Textbook God has used this teaching method perhaps more than any other. He has recorded case after case, to teach us how He encounters men, to teach us what He wants from this encounter. It is as though He has given us access to a lavish selection of case histories, so that every aspect of truth is demon- strated. Here is the greatest ward-round any student can undertake. All are cases needing treatment, and every aspect of their need, as of their treatment, may here be studied in the official clinical records. Tempera- ture charts? X-rays and blood counts? Autopsies? Yes, they are all there, even a number of fatal cases, with the full relevant post-mortem findings. Complications? Oh, yes. All the complications. Some of the cases are recorded only as the complication—like empyema, where you must pre-suppose the causative pneumonia.

Yes, they are there, one after another. That is why the Bible is not just a history book; rather is it a *case-history* book. And as you thus read it you may come to see better what God has in mind for your life. And wonder of wonders, your name (and mine) may in the ages to come be found in the Lamb's Book of Life, as one of the Successful Cases.

In the following pages, I am going to assume the duties of a clinical tutor, and take you through the records of four of these case-histories that God has preserved for us. The only reason I can offer for claiming such a responsibility and privilege is that I have myself spent many years now in the company of the Teacher Himself, and have, I believe, learnt enough of Him, from Him, to be able to explain something of His way with men.

The first case we shall be studying is that of Pharaoh. In human history, he is probably Rameses II, whose mummy is still to be seen in Cairo Museum today. But in God's Case-book he is the main example of a man who refuses to surrender his own human will to the claim of the authority of God. The Bible always maintains that every one of us has been endowed, by virtue of the mere fact of being man, with the notion that his life is entirely his own: that he may do with it just what he likes. Every man is equipped with the self-assertive desire to subdue the world, to have dominion over it. And when he then finds his human will confronted by the divine will, when his creatureliness is challenged by his Creator, God, man is on the hot-spot. He now sees and recognizes himself for what he really is. Rebel, enemy, sinner, disobedient, alien— these are some of the words used in the Bible to describe this pride, this arrogant reaction, which, from being his noblest quality, now becomes in man a most deadly disease-process.

In the following dramatic, exciting, yet bleak and tragic tale, we shall see this king refuse to humble himself before God. We shall meet Pharaoh while he is still hardly aware of the fact that there is any of this disease-process in him at all, and we shall watch the awareness grow and grow, until finally he is completely convinced that there is no single part of him that is unaffected. And we shall surely be stirred and awed as we discover that this is just what Pharaoh wants. Yes, it suits him. Nothing else will satisfy him. And most stirring and awesome of all is the discovery that this is what God Himself has been entirely aware of all the time. 'It is for this cause I raised you up,' St. Paul reminds us, is God's own comment on Pharaoh. Let me assure you that I, too, find this a terrifying case-history.

And then we jump about seven centuries to another great king—none other than Nebuchadnezzar, king of Babylon, probably the greatest king of all history. And again we see God moving in and challenging this human giant. We hold our breath, scarcely daring to watch, lest the misery of Pharaoh should be repeated on this enormous human scale, only to find instead that the exact opposite has taken place. The great Nebuchadnezzar, with all his glory, and his Hanging Gardens, and scholarship, and might, is finally bowing humbly and submissively under the love-lightened yoke of God. Nebuchadnezzar, the son of Nabopolassar, king of Babylon, 'converts', to be re-born Nebuchadnezzar, a son of the most high God, King of heaven.

These are two mighty stories, case-histories of the most striking order. As we finish looking into them, we shall surely begin to see that we are all in our tiny, 'common man' way doing what one of these two did, in his vast, 'big-shot' way. We shall begin to realize that their stories are exactly like ours, but on a larger and more obvious social scale. We, too, are either 'hardening our hearts', or on the way to serving and adoring the 'most high God'.

Most of us, I expect, have listened at some time or other to Handel's great oratorio *Messiah*, and have been moved as the rich, resonant voice of the bass-baritone has declaimed the recitative:

> 'Thus saith the Lord of Hosts; Yet once a little
> while, and I will shake the heavens, and the
> earth, the sea, and the dry land; and I will
> shake all nations.'

As you listen you cannot fail to catch the great burning passion of the prophet Haggai himself. Then the
sudden glow of hope and pleasure as the swelling
announcement answers:

> 'The desire of all nations shall come'

is chilled by the question:

> 'But who may abide the day of His coming?'

and it is then altogether swept away in the thunder
and lightning of the aria,

> 'For He is like a refiner's fire.'

Yes, the voice and skill of a great singer, the music
of Handel, the spiritual imagination of the prophet, all
are here directed to proclaiming the tremendous truth
which we shall relive as we study the case-histories of
Pharaoh and Nebuchadnezzar. We shall see God shaking the heavens, the earth, the nations. We shall see
these two men tremble at the appearance of the Lord.
We shall see the refining fire sweeping into these
people's lives, and the lives of their nations as they fall
subdued before the Lord of hosts.

Surely, then, a huge question will begin to form in
our minds, as we watch this awesome spectacle. The
question of *Why?* The question of purpose, the reason
for it all.

This is the question that I, and all my fellow-doctors,
hear more than any other single question. 'Doctor,
why has this happened to me?'

We soon come to recognize that quite often the
question is really, 'Doctor, can you simply explain the
mechanism?' And because we are trained in Medical

Schools, where the body machinery is in part understood, we can very often help the patient to understand just what bearing has been running too hot, what cog has slipped, what fuel-line has blocked. Yes, that is usually all that is needed. The patient then goes away happily enough, relieved to find that it is only a small bearing or an unimportant cog or a subsidiary fuel-line; or, perhaps, he will go off more composed, knowing that while it is a main bearing, an essential cog, an irreplaceable fuel-line, his doctor will still be beside him to relieve his pain and lead him to the vast resources of our modern technological skills.

Yes. That is the common question, and the easy one to answer. But sometimes we hear the other question, the big question. '*Why?* Never mind the machinery. I know how it's caused. Don't go over that. But *why?* What have I done to deserve this? Why should I have to get polio right in the middle of my university course? . . . Why should my little boy be killed? . . . Why should my wife get cancer? . . . Why did my coronary artery occlude?' And I must bow my head, humbled, as I answer, 'I'm trained only in a Medical School. I can tell you only *how* it happened. If you want to know *why* this has happened, you shouldn't ask your Doctor. You should ask your Maker.'

This is the really big question. The answer to this is the thing of which all Philosophy is properly made. This is the deep, yearning search of the very heart of man in every culture through all the ages. This is the explanation of what St. Paul calls the 'futility' or 'vanity' of creatureliness. We will forget the *Whence?* of the past, we will take a chance on the *Whither?* of the future, if only we can have explained to us the *Why?* of the present. If only God would tell us *Why?*

Now I believe most strongly that God has in fact told us more about this answer than He has about anything else at all. The Bible is simply full of it. Even the Whence, the story of man's origin, is told in the Bible only in terms of the purpose of man's being at all. Think of what endless nonsense has been bleated

forth in explanation or criticism of the first three
chapters of the book of Genesis because of the obsessional insistence of the modern Western mind that
everything must be interpreted in terms of What or
How. And certainly in the Bible the Whither, the
statement of man's destiny, is meaningful only if it can
be seen in its proper relationship of being the fulfil-
ment of the experiences of the Today of Life. It is never
a Bible idea to think that 'the ages to come' can be
detached from the 'today' of this life on earth.

Yes. The Bible is simply full of this great answer.
This answer, which the great Greek philosophers tried
to guess with their concepts of the duality of man and
his 'immortal soul'; this answer, which St. Paul reminds us was unknown even to Isaiah—this, he says,
'God has revealed to us through his Holy Spirit'. This
is the great central truth of all the Bible, the truth now
blazing in the dazzling clarity of the One who is the
Light of the world, the One whose name is Truth.

Come with me again, if you will, as we look in the
second part of this book at the stories of two men
whose lives have been recorded so that we may learn
this truth. And because God Himself has not hesitated
to tell us both sides of the truth, we shall again be
looking first at the account of a man who chose darkness. We shall be given something of that dreadful,
terrible insight that God alone has fully, as He allows
us a fleeting glimpse into the inner make-up of a man
who, like Pharaoh, looked full into the face of God
and then preferred his own human littleness. This
record will show us, much more than did the story of
Pharaoh, just what goes on inside the very character
of a man who rejects the love of God. As we study this
case we shall realize something of the blackness that
God has never been reluctant or embarrassed in ad-
mitting. From this story we may come to understand
the intensity of St. Paul's argument: 'It is the God
who said, "Let light shine out of darkness", who has
shone in our hearts to give the light of the knowledge
of the glory of God in the face of Christ.' Studying this

man will surely make us feel the deep burning urgency
in the voice of Jesus as He pleaded: 'Never be afraid
of those who can kill the body but are powerless to kill
the soul. Far better to stand in awe of the One who
has the power to destroy body and soul in the fires of
destruction.'

In this our third case-history, we shall see God meet
with Saul, a delightful enough fellow, if ever there was
one. A rich, handsome, eligible young farmer, is the
way to describe him. This intelligent, industrious
young man is no more bothered about God than any
other successful young man in Sydney, London, or
Timbuktu can be expected to be. But God is concerned about him. And we shall surely watch spell-
bound as we see God's encounter with him. It is a story
that makes a modern T.V. thriller look like the tiny
tot's slumber corner. We shall see him picked up by
the hand of God, and his whole life and character
transformed. And what we see going on inside the
man, in his character and personality structure, is
surely one of the most dreadful things ever recorded.
We shall see a cheerful, reliable, resourceful young
man dying finally as a bitter, cynical, cruel, broken-
hearted suicide.

I remember once hearing a fellow student ask a professor whether he had ever seen a patient die of in-
fection by vibrio—the toxic little cholera germ that
can kill a man by exhaustion in twenty-four hours; and
I was particularly impressed by the almost awesome
way in which the professor replied, 'No. And I hope
to God I never do.' I feel like that whenever I read
or think about Saul. As I ponder over this story of
Saul, I want to fall on my knees, and cover my head
and cry, 'Oh God, never, never let me be like that.
Please, oh please, save me from the end of Saul.'

And even as I pray this, with all the sincerity I
know, the other big question starts thundering in my
mind. But what then? What if I do avoid the fate of
Saul? Suppose I do agree to give in to God, suppose I
am 'crucified with Christ', as St. Paul describes it, sup-

pose I do become 'like a grain of wheat, and fall into the ground and die', as Jesus Himself expresses it? Suppose all that, then what do I get out of it? Do I get anything? What will God do to me? Will He just shove me around; or just leave me alone; or rub me out; or gobble me up; or just fix me up all pretty-pretty, like a poodle dog in the lap of a dowager in a swanky limousine? Come on. What is the answer to that?

This tremendous question is answered by at least three stories in the Bible. In fact in some sense it is the answer to all the stories of the Bible, as it is the answer to all the stories of the men of God in all the years.

We are going back over four thousand years, to one of the most human, as well as one of the longest of all the stories in the Bible, to learn this most wonderful of all answers. 'Oh God, *my* God, why has this happened to me?' And we shall smile a little as we cry a little as we are thrilled altogether as we watch it work out in the life of Joseph. We shall learn from him in whom the end is seen, what we so long to know for ourselves in whom the end is not yet. We shall learn from Joseph, the mixed-up kid, the farmer's son, the Prime Minister of Egypt, a man of God, just what it is that happened when 'God showed him steadfast love'.

CHAPTER TWO

A FATAL CASE

CHRISTIANS declare that God made the world. They also say that He made every other thing in existence, and that having made all this, He now operates it so that it does exactly as He plans it and wills it.

If you are a philosopher, you will be dismayed by such a categorical statement as this, because in one sense it puts you out of business. All the fine arguments and homilies and what-not in the great matter of Determinism are entirely answered in one pat sentence—'Everything is God-determined.'

Now if your blood-pressure has not reached danger levels and destroyed any hope of your reading on, I should like you to look carefully with me into this tremendous claim, and see if we can discover how it works out in actual life.

The most obvious thing is that it wouldn't amount to much of a problem if it were not for us. A million years ago, say, when there were primates evolving something of a hominid pattern, but nothing on the world we should seriously consider as 'men', the statement would need little challenge. We would see a world with plants and animals struggling for existence, each making a desperate biological attempt to sustain and reproduce its own life-story. And we might well say, that if there is a God who made it all, and that's the way He wanted it, it's okay by us. We may not quite understand or even approve of the idea, but we should at least be deeply impressed with the sheer wonder of the mechanisms of existence as we are now learning them in the sciences.

But when we come to man, to the twentieth century, to ourselves today, we are well advised to call out, 'Wait! Wait! This needs a bit of thought.' Because we are sure that while God may be having some influence, and we may even admit it's quite a big influence on human affairs, that is really all it is. Why, look at Professor So-and-so; and Dr. Thingummy. And in fact I know lots of fellows, from Ph.D.s to dockers and dustmen, who don't care two brass buttons about God, and what's more don't mind saying so, either politely or rudely, according to the manners their mothers taught them! Some of them say the very idea of God is simply wishful thinking, and lots of psychologists teach that the whole story of God and religion is just one part of the mechanism of mind and personality, and that's that.

Then how do we add all this up, and say that every single thing is planned and calculated and known and chosen, and all the rest? Just what on earth does Jesus mean when He says that every hair on our head has a number on it? Surely this is fantasy, euphemism, and is simply outside the limits of truth as we live and observe ourselves and our fellows.

Good. If you think that way, and are serious in your criticism, then I would ask you to read on, because you will find the following story arresting and enthralling.

But if you think there is no problem, and the solution is as simple as kiss-your-hand, then stop reading and ask for your money back, because you're still in the kindergarten; and this is for grown-ups.

The hub of the whole matter may be expressed in the simple truth, that God made you, and me ('man', that is), with a particular slant which is best described as a desire, an intention, to run our own lives. And aren't we all a little bit bothered at adolescence, and by adolescents, as the biological capacity to be grown-up, to be ourselves, is in conflict with the fact that we are dependent on mum and dad, and have to fit in with society? Isn't it true that we all get quite a kick out of the idea that we are supposed to be fruitful, to multiply and fill the earth, to have dominion over it, to subdue it? Sure, that is this tremendous drive that we call sex: that is the great burning aggressiveness that is in some measure churning away inside even the

merest worm of a man: that is what it really all adds
up to.

That is the easy end of the doctrine. That is the end
we like. That makes our ambition, our self-determina-
tion—whatever name we like to give this aim in life—
the correct and proper thing we inwardly feel it to
be.

But the other end of the doctrine packs a terrific
punch. It is a knock-out in every sense of the word.
For Christians say that, having made man like that,
standing (or wanting to stand) fairly on his little back-
legs, God then deliberately and definitely steps into
each man's life, and asks him to hand over to God the
whole authority of his human existence. In other
words, God asks man to sell out to Him, in terms of
aim, or will, or whatever it is that makes a man think
of himself as first person singular, 'I'.

And, says the Christian, God asks this in such a
manner and with such pressure that the man must
give a definite answer. Man is forced into the position
where he has to say clearly—'God', or 'Mammon'; 'You
are Master', or 'I am still boss'. And the Christian goes
on just that little bit further, to imply, rather than to
state, that the whole of the course of life can be understood as being a single experience, in which this one
answer is the entire thing.

I think I can see the furrows creasing your thought-
ful brow as you ponder this. Yesterday, when I worked
at that essay . . . last night, when I took Agatha to
the pictures . . . this morning, when I had two eggs
with my bacon . . . today, spent in conference with
the boss . . . how on earth can that sort of thing have
anything whatever to do with serving God or not serving God? Isn't that what I'm supposed to think about
in church; or when I'm in a more pensive mood, out
fishing, or something like that? Is that what you mean?
Is God directly concerned with and in these everyday
'human' experiences, which fill up most hours of most
days?

The answer is yes. That is exactly what *is* meant.

Look at it this way. God, as Maker, as Planner and
Creator, has planned an appointment between Himself
and each man He has made, including you and me. He
doesn't invite us to keep the appointment. He tells us.
And then, when the appointment is kept, He asks us,
simply and clearly, to decide for all time, and for all
that succeeds time, what our intention is: is it to carry
on, going our own way, choosing our own will? or is it
to convert, and go His way, choosing His will? And
the time of the appointment is the today of human
life.

In His Textbook, God has been good enough to
record for us a few cases of this encounter, stories from
which the simplest mind may learn just what it is all
about. And He has been doubly good, in that He has
recorded the sort of cases which highlight the whole
picture. If your story, or mine, were there, it wouldn't
tell anyone much at all. We are too ordinary. At any
rate I am. So God has picked out lives etched in deep
black and white, with motives and methods easy to
see.

The first story we shall look at is a tremendous one.
It is a tale of kings, national disasters, falling dynas-
ties, and man versus God. That is not because God is
a showman, but because the man He was to interview
was that sort of man; not that he was really big, but
his social setting was immense. He was himself, as I
think you'll come to see, a rather petty little chap: not
good at all at making up his mind, and yet never prepared to stop and think. He was the sort of man that
writers in *Punch* would place in a public service job
and there show him to be a thorough little 'red tape'
nuisance. And sadly enough, he was born in a setting
which taught him that he was in fact God, that he was
truly divine. He was a king over a huge nation with
an absolute despotism of a fairy-tale pattern. And
somehow, in this setting, God was to meet this man,
and from him, as from all of us, obtain the answer
to the authority of life. This man has to be shown, in

spite of this odd cultural background, that there is a
God in heaven who asks to be obeyed. It really does
take a lot of manœuvring.

And the balloon is up. Pharaoh, king of all Egypt,
is to keep his appointment with God.

God has been preparing, of course. God knows the
future, and is never at a loss for the next move. Man
is the one who tries to buck and dodge. And God had
been at work preparing His personnel. The main
human agent in the story was a Hebrew baby who had
been born during the reign of a previous Pharaoh.
The Hebrews were then slaves of the Egyptians, and
were located in a district called Goshen. The baby's
mother had been persuaded by God to take her little
boy, and place him in a wicker basket, daubed with
bitumen, and float this tiny craft with its little passen-
ger on the River Nile. And sure enough, for of course
God knew the currents and winds and so on, just as
He knew every plan and action of every member of
Pharaoh's household, there was the little ark almost at
the feet of one of the Egyptian princesses, as she was
down at the sacred River Nile for her daily ablutions.

In these days of birth-control and limited families,
with our strong social convictions about monogamy
and incest, the reaction of the princess is as unexpected
to us as it was fully known to God. Any half-wit could
see at a glance that this was obviously a Hebrew baby,
afloat in an obviously home-made boat. And so could
the princess. But this was the particular princess God
had chosen to be there on just that particular occasion.
What of the king's edict to eliminate the Hebrew in-
fants? What of the social repercussions if an Egyptian
princess were seen with a Hebrew babe? What, in fact,
of the rather invidious place of a princess of the divine
royal blood at all, in a court where brother-sister and
father-daughter marriages were acceptable, and where
a princess might well find marriage and family an even
greater emotional gamble than it is in our modern
Western world?

I don't know just what went on in the mind of the

princess, as she saw the tiny ark with its even tinier
load: the feeling of womanly pity which was her first
reaction immediately strengthened into the bond of
motherly possessiveness as she gave orders for the infant to be cared for, to be given to his natural mother
to act as foster-mother for the princess herself, to be
brought into the palace as her own adopted son. I
don't know, and you don't know just how this all came
about in her mind. Our clinical experience in psychological behaviour patterns can easily enough be tied in
with the sociological data we may derive from the
studies of the Egyptologists. But we can't say we know
the answer—the deductions we so make may be very
wide of the mark. For God has not recorded this
account of His activities in the lives of people just so
that we may brush up our psychology. This is not
intended as a starter for a brilliant exposé of historical
characters as a basis for a Ph.D. thesis. It is not written
as an account of the inner working of the mind of an
Egyptian princess—it is an account of the inner working of the mind of God Himself, as He placed the baby
at the feet of the princess.

Yes. Any half-wit could see that this was a Hebrew
baby afloat in an obviously home-made boat. But to the
princess here now was a little boy given her by the
sacred Nile. Surely a son of the Gods, a child for the
palace. And Moses, the baby in the bulrushes, the Hebrew infant, is brought up in luxury as a son of the
Pharaohs.

And then Moses is sent away for forty years, in which
time the Pharaoh we are to look at comes to the throne.
And I may as well make something clear now, as later.
When you come to read this tale in the book of
Exodus, you will notice how this particular story is
recorded, up to this point, as essentially Moses' story.
It is his record of encounter with God. But now the
story moves very noticeably to Pharaoh. It is still part
of Moses' story, of course. But we can follow it more
easily from now on, as the story of Pharaoh and his
appointment with God.

God made the next move. He always makes all the
moves, while man tries to hide. God sent Moses back
to Egypt, to conduct the interview for Him. 'Moses, go
to Pharaoh and tell him what I want.' Moses has an
I.Q. of about 160-plus, and knows his Pharaohs. And
he knows his Hebrews, who seem to have an average
I.Q. of about 70.

Moses was nonplussed. 'Oh, God, send somebody
else. I'm not the talking type.' Moses was to learn, but
he hadn't then learned, that if God asks a man to do
something, it is up to God to provide the equipment
needed. Moses, the greatest man probably in all human
history, was still to learn that. But again, this is Moses'
story and it will take him another forty years to find
it all out. God said: 'Then take Aaron, your elder
brother. He is a great talker. He can do the talking
for you. And Moses, remember this, when you talk to
Pharaoh, you will be God to him, and Aaron will be
your prophet.' Of course this is simple enough really,
as Pharaoh knew that Moses was divine, having come
out of the Nile; and yet I doubt whether Moses understood what even the most simply taught Christian today
knows: that God lives in His people, and, as He in-
dwells them, He is perpetually meeting with the
Pharaohs around them.

And now Moses and Aaron, his prophet, are on their
way to tell Pharaoh what God wants. Note particularly
the fair, decent way God goes about the whole thing.
He sends the only man who is capable of entering the
Egyptian royal household and talking to the king at
his own level. And the matter for decision is more
noteworthy still. God did not come to Pharaoh asking
for a change in the pattern in the national religion.
He did not ask Pharaoh to reconsider some of his views
on polytheism. No! God did not speak in that language at all. God asked something that fitted Pharaoh
exactly. 'The God of Israel says, "Let My people go,
that they may hold a feast to Me in the wilderness."'
That is a simple direct request for one God to make
to another. It is a matter of administration, which is

Pharaoh's role, and where a clear-cut decision is readily made. Pharaoh pauses only a minute and gives his answer.

'Who is this Yahweh, God of Israel, that I should take any notice of what He says, and let Israel go? I do not know Yahweh. And in any case, I won't let them go.'

Moses is not to be shaken off so abruptly. He knows God—had he not met Him in the wilderness? Moses probably knows more about God than any other man is to know for fifteen hundred years. 'Your Majesty, the God of the Hebrews has met us; and He asks us to go and worship Him. If we fail (and He wants us to go for only three days in all) He may punish us.'

Pharaoh is only half listening. But the half he does hear is the half he doesn't like one little bit! Who are these Hebrews, that they are more worried by what their tin-pot God says than by what *I* say? He turned to the two men and spat back his answer. 'Moses and Aaron! Why do you stop the people working? There are too many of you Hebrews, and you are just loafing. Get back to your work!'

As he thought it over, Pharaoh was more and more annoyed. God has just that knack. His voice in human affairs has been aptly described as 'alive and active; it cuts more keenly than any two-edged sword: it strikes through to the place where soul and spirit meet, to the innermost intimacies of a man's being: it exposes the very thoughts and motives of a man's heart. No creature has any cover from the sight of God.' Pharaoh, God is after you!

His blood-pressure still round the danger mark, Pharaoh whistled up his heads of departments and the works foremen. 'Listen to this! Those lazy Hebrews want to go and have time off to sacrifice to their God! They are loafers. Tomorrow don't give them any straw to make their bricks, but still make them produce the same tally of bricks. Make it tough for the lying scoundrels. Them and their religion and their God!'

Pharaoh, you don't know much yet, but the first

lesson has been taught, and you have learned it. God sees to it that you do. It has shown you that you are up against God Himself. And even though you have as yet no idea of what that means, you do know that to Moses, at least, God is greater than you. Moses rates God ahead of Pharaoh.

Moses meanwhile is in a spot of bother with the Hebrews. No straw, but the same number of bricks! The foremen of the Hebrew workmen went to the Egyptian bosses to complain. And got whipped! They came back, limping, moaning, complaining more bitterly than ever. 'Moses, you great big nuisance! Now see the mess we are in! We hope God cracks down on you for making us so hated by the Egyptians. You have put a sword in their hands to kill us.'

Moses prayed, and God told him that it was as He planned. God is not caught out—Pharaoh has still to be met. 'Moses, you go back and tell Pharaoh again what I want. And Moses, I know he won't listen to you, or agree; but tell him none the less. And he will get more and more set in his opposition—and all the people of Egypt will know that I am God. Now go, and do all the things I have taught you.'

I think Moses was more grim, but I am certain he was more confident the next day as he met the king again. 'Let My people go three days into the wilderness to worship Me.' This is to become a sort of chorus in the story. Pharaoh heard it again, and I can see his little mind wriggling. Moses was way ahead of him in brains, in experience, in personality. But Pharaoh sees his escape. 'Yes,' he replied. 'But what proof can you give that this God of yours is really worth the slightest attention?' Fair enough, Pharaoh. If you are to obey God this once, who is to say where it will end? It may not end. It will not end! Isn't that the real trouble? Three days off to worship—this time. More, perhaps, the next. And there is no end. Before it is over you won't be king at all—God will be. 'Yes, Moses. Prove yourselves. Prove it by working a miracle.'

God always plays fair. If Pharaoh is the sort of man

who needs magic and signs to strengthen the argument, then God is gracious enough to put on the signs. In a scientific, materialist age like ours, that sort of thing is just confusing, and we rarely find God speaking in that way nowadays. But to Pharaoh that was just playing the game fairly.

Moses signalled to Aaron, his prophet—and Aaron threw his rod on the ground. It became a snake! Pharaoh was impressed, but not much. This was common enough party magic in Egypt. He called in his magicians, and put it to them. They all tossed their rods on the ground and they all turned to snakes. Pharaoh grinned. Poor old Moses. Pulling out the stuff he learned in the University of Memphis forty or fifty years ago.

And then Aaron's rod swallowed up the Egyptians' rods!

This is real post-graduate stuff. Pharaoh swallows hard. I must get some of my better men to go abroad to take some higher degrees, and learn this one. 'No, Moses. I won't let you go!'

Pharaoh, do you see what you are doing? This God is just above you. His 'magic' is a notch ahead of yours. Not so much that you are overwhelmed, which is not what He wants; but far enough for you to see that He is in fact ahead. You asked for a test of magic, didn't you? And you have been answered, haven't you? What is that you say, Pharaoh? And Pharaoh shut his tight lips tighter still. 'He hardened his heart . . .'

The next morning, as Pharaoh was going down to the sacred Nile, Moses was standing there waiting for him. 'Pharaoh, God has said to tell you that He still wants His people to go three days into the wilderness to worship Him. You have not obeyed Him. Aaron!'— and Moses swung round on his elder brother—'Take your rod and stretch out your hand over the waters of the Nile. Let it turn to blood!'

Aaron's rod moved over the water, and it turned to blood! The fish died, the water was undrinkable. Pharaoh stood there, his servants all around him. He called for his magicians. They looked up their records, found the chapter 'Water: How to Turn to Blood' and did the same. I have often chuckled at this. Surely the real test would have been to ask the magicians to look up 'Blood. How to Turn Back to Water'. But Pharaoh is a weak and not very intelligent man, and he doesn't think as well as that. He is under pressure concerning his will and the will of God, and he doesn't want to make it a matter of rational decision. Who ever really did? Isn't the atheist the most desperate wishful thinker imaginable?

Pharaoh went back to his palace, to drink champagne and lager and schnapps, no doubt.

A week passed. God doesn't rush men. He owns time. He made it. At the end of the week, Moses met Pharaoh again. Again the same chorus. 'Let My people go!' This time Pharaoh is told that refusal means frogs. Frogs in the houses, frogs in the ovens, frogs in the beds, frogs everywhere. And Pharaoh settled for frogs!

Pharaoh called up his magicians again. 'Do the same!' They did the same. They called up frogs. I must say that at that particular time in their history, I think anyone could have had frogs for the asking!

This time God got Pharaoh in a sore spot. Men must never be allowed to think that life is just a sort of game. It is in fact something that involves the very life (and even the death) of God Himself. Pharaoh, you may scoff at snakes out of rods, water into blood. You say you can take it! You think you can match your toughness against God's strength! But frogs. Ugh! Pharaoh is allergic to frogs. The A. A. Milne of that day would have needed more than a little bit of butter for the royal slice of bread to hide the slice of frog that had got itself baked in the dough!

Pharaoh came to Moses, this time. Pharaoh was shaken, beaten. 'Moses, you win. Would you ask your God to get rid of the frogs?' I am sure he had already tried to get his magicians to clear out the frogs, but of course men can only do what God allows them.

Moses' answer is delightful. 'Certainly. When would

you like it?' 'Tomorrow' came the answer like a shot.
'That is all right. Tomorrow, if you say so.' And in
the morning all the frogs died; the people heaped
them up in huge stacks, and the whole country stank!
Only the frogs in the Nile were left alive—a good
enough place for frogs.

Pharaoh, what about your promise to let the people
go to worship? You named the day to clear the frogs.
Shall we name the day to go to worship?

'But when Pharaoh saw that there was a respite, he
hardened his heart, and would not listen to them.'

Moses called to Aaron to stretch out his rod, and
the ground became alive with gnats. Gnats were on
man and beast. The magicians tried this one too, but
were beaten. They were white-lipped as they faced
Pharaoh. 'This is the finger of God,' they said shakily.
Pharaoh cursed them under his breath for the craven
fools they were. Gnats! Bah! It takes more than a
few gnat-bites to beat me!

Moses came to the king again. 'Let My people go.
Otherwise it is to be flies. And by the way, the flies
will not be in the land of Goshen, where the Hebrews
are! What do you say, Pharaoh?' And Pharaoh settled
for flies.

What a funny thing a man is, when you look at him
from this vantage point. Beaten, and knowing he is
beaten, and refusing to give up. And always with the
simple rational undercurrent of argument that makes
him know he is a fool. And Pharaoh hated flies even
more than he hated frogs. The same sort of psychology,
no doubt. Flies everywhere—except among the Hebrews. Pharaoh called Moses again. 'You win,' he said.
'Go and worship in the borders of my kingdom.'

'That will not do,' said Moses. 'We are shepherd
people, and we will do things that your people will
hate. They despise sheep, as a very abominable beast.
No, we will do what Yahweh says, and nothing less.'

Pharaoh, don't you know yet that God is not to be
kept to a border, given limits to fit into? We are not
here to tell Him what He should be satisfied with.

Yes, Pharaoh knew that, and that was why he suggested it. Must he come round and give God the full payment? And the flies were buzzing, and he was sick with the sound and sight of them. 'All right, all right, all right! You win. Only get rid of the flies for me. Please, no more flies. And ask your God not to take you too far away.'

So Moses prayed, and God sent a strong wind that blew all the flies into the Red Sea, and the historian says 'not one remained'. And Pharaoh took a deep breath, found that he could do so without coughing over any flies, and called the deal off. 'God, get me out of this slit-trench alive and I'll be a better man.' 'God, let my little boy live, and I will go to church again.' 'God, listen to me, and I will listen to you.' How often has this been the cry of Pharaohs through the ages. 'Call a National Day of Prayer.'—'Pray for rain.'—'Pray for peace.' And the music goes round and round, and the heart is hardened. Call it off. It was only an emotional experience! Ha! Ha! I was only a boy, of course—and didn't know much better. . . .

'Pharaoh, God will send a plague on the live-stock of your land. It will not happen in the land of Goshen. It will begin tomorrow.'

Pharaoh sent out scouts. Yes, his animals were going down in a pitiful way; and the Hebrew flocks were immune. And he shut his mouth tight, and snapped his fingers at Moses. 'I can take it. What are a few herds and stock to me? I am Pharaoh. I won't give way an inch.'

Moses and Aaron took handfuls of ashes from the kilns, and threw the ashes into the air. And as the dust blew away over the land, the people came out in sores. Boils all over them. The magicians were covered with boils. All the Egyptians were sore with boils. (Of course today we would like to know a lot more about the boils. We would like to know the causative organism, its pathogenicity, its antibiotic sensitivity, and a whole stack of things that aren't told us. But this is not recorded as a study in Bacteriology or Parasitology, any more than the frogs are a study in Biology or the water-into-blood is a study in Chemistry. Some day we will be told all the facts. This is a study in man versus God.) And Pharaoh poulticed his boils and ached with the toxic reaction and screamed 'NO!'

Moses went back to Pharaoh yet again. He was stern and doing the talking himself, now. Never mind Aaron this time. 'Look, Pharaoh. Can't you see reason? God could just as easily have sent you a plague that would have killed you as any of these other things He has done. You still think you can exalt your little self against God. Then note this well. Tomorrow I will call down hail such as has never been seen before. If you or your beasts or your slaves are out in the hail, they will be killed. And remember this, Pharaoh: God says, "I have only let you live to show My power, so that My name shall be exalted in the earth." Tomorrow, it will be hail.'

It was the hail that did it. God doesn't take any delight in just sending hail, that breaks down the crops, beats down the live-stock, kills the men who venture out in it. God is not a sadist. He is not a masochist. God is love. But because Love is so big, so strong, so good, Love can never be stopped just by sentiment and emotion. To love is to will the Best—and the Best that God has planned must have a 'capital'. It is something as great as Himself. Yes, Pharaoh, the hail is necessary.

Many people find this very, very hard to understand. 'God, why can't I just be comfortable? Why can't You simply keep life convenient? In fact, God, I'd settle for cash straight out, and then I could buy enough comfort and convenience to get by.' No, it must be hail.

There are two very lovely things told in the narrative at this point. They will surely help answer two questions you should by now have been asking. Firstly, what about all the simple people? If this is the story of God versus Pharaoh, it seems most unfair. You say that God has been doing all this to speak to Pharaoh? Then it is monstrous to send blood and frogs and gnats and flies and boils on all the other people, kill off their

live-stock, and now lash them with hail. The answer is
given, and it is simple: We are told that in all this,
and out of all this, some of the Egyptian people had
come to believe in God, to serve Him. And that means
that He is now the One to whom they give the obedience and authority of life. And because of that, they
heard His word about the hail—and to hear is to obey.
They brought their herds and slaves in out of the open.
You see, God had been speaking to them, in their own
way of life, speaking a language they understood.

And the other question is answered—the question of
'Why all this sheer destruction?' The answer is, that it
is *not* sheer destruction. It is revelation. Sometimes
(and this is one of the times) it is necessary to speak this
way. It is the revelation that is necessary—not the destruction itself. The hail was destructive all right—as
down went the flax and barley, with the men and beasts
who ventured out. 'But the wheat and spelt were not
ruined, for they were late in coming up.' Love is always
like that. God is always like that. He feels the pain and
the suffering, Himself, and keeps it to the smallest possible area of experience. If it is possible, God will spare
the wheat and spelt. He will see to it that they are late
in coming up. But Love must never become small and
sentimental, and just dodge pain.

Pharaoh, what do you think of the hail?

Pharaoh is beaten. He is trembling and awed. He
comes calling for Moses again. 'I have sinned. Your
God is right. I and my people are in the wrong.'

Yes, Pharaoh has now met God fairly, and knows it.
It is not now a story of party magic, of post-graduate
degrees. It is not just the luck of the game, the toss of
the coin, the prizes in the lottery of life. It is God. It
is purpose. It is the very mind and will of the Maker
Himself. And I am up against the One who is always
the greater, always above.

'Moses, your God wins. I will give Him best. Please
ask Him to stop the hail, and you can go and worship
as He wants.'

Moses prayed, and the hail stopped. And Pharaoh

took it all back again. Of course he did. He was still
Pharaoh. The call of God to men is to cease being
themselves, to cease being the 'I' of life, and to recognize that He is Himself all life. And this is just the
very thing that Pharaoh could now see clearly that he
did not want. He had been squeezed into recognizing
his littleness, his contrariness; and with seeing the
'aboveness' of God; but no man can be squeezed into
converting his 'I' into the 'Thou' of obedience of faith.
That is the one thing in man which must for ever
remain inviolate. That is the one, tiny, but altogether
real, freedom man possesses. That is the wonder of all
this material universe: a mere fourteen hundred grams
of brain, plus associated physiology, which has yet
within it the marvel of being free to be self-determin-
ing, when truly confronted with the supreme will and
freedom of God.

Pharaoh, get your feet well set! Balance yourself
carefully on the facts you have seen. Look steadily on
the One you have been talking with. And tell Him
now to His Face, what you fully and finally say.

'But when Pharaoh saw that the rain and hail and
thunder had ceased, he sinned yet again, and hardened
his heart. . . . He did not let the people go.'

I don't know your thoughts, as you read this. But I
can tell you some of mine. This is a story I have read
many times and know much of it almost off by heart.
And yet I confess to a lump in my throat, and a leaden
weight in my heart, as I sit here writing this. I see
something of the utter sadness and desolation of a poor
tiny man who is in open and declared rebellion against
God. Pharaoh, how can you do it? Is your own way
so very good that it is worth that? Is anything at all
worth that? Pharaoh, you are going into darkness.
Outer darkness. Have you thought it over carefully? Do
you want to reconsider it? Is this your real answer?

'The heart of Pharaoh was hardened, and he did not
let the people of Israel go.'

And that is the end. It is all over. Another human
personality has looked into the will of God, and said

'No'. Finally, clearly. And we turn the page to see whose story comes next, to find it is still Pharaoh. Yes, Pharaoh still. The same Pharaoh who has just said, 'God is right. I am in the wrong. But I still won't do it.' How good God is. How long-suffering. How truly great.

Moses and Aaron went back to Pharaoh again, on the same simple, monotonous theme. I wonder if Pharaoh was surprised. He thought he had ended the episode. He thought the interview was closed. Pharaoh, can't you yet see that it is God who opens the interview, and He who closes it? 'Pharaoh, let My people go, that they may serve Me. You have till tomorrow to decide. For tomorrow I will bring locusts into your country in a way you have never seen before. Every blade and leaf will be stripped in your land, and your houses, even, will be filled with them tomorrow. Goodbye.' His courtiers come to the king, despairingly. Words that have probably never been said to a Pharaoh, by a mere man, a mere adviser, just burst from them. 'Sir, this is sheer madness!' 'This man is ruining us.' 'For heaven's sake, why not let them go? Three days off work won't break us, but a bit more of this will.' 'Be sensible, Sir. Stop this shambles.'

But Pharaoh knows this is not, and never has been, a matter of simple economics. It is not the loss of time and work he is concerned with. It is the loss of himself. That is his problem. He would rather lose his whole kingdom than that. 'Moses,' he calls out; 'come and talk this over. I'll let you go, but you must leave the children.' (How similar, in reverse, to the twentieth-century Western man. From him the reply is: 'Leave me alone. I'll send the kids to Sunday School—that should satisfy you, God.')

Pharaoh, do you remember a few days ago, saying you were wrong, that you had sinned? Are you now going to start trying to make terms again? Can't you remember that terms with God must always be His terms, not yours? Moses said what he will always say—what God always has said: 'Our men will go, our wives

will go, our children will go, our flocks and herds will
go.' God doesn't confront men with an offer to share
the load of life. His call is to surrender the life itself,
together with its load.

'Then you'll never go. That is the thing I'll never
come at. Get out.'

And the locusts came. They cleaned the country bare
of everything that looked like being alive. They filled
the houses. They took the lot.

And poor Pharaoh tried the same old dodge he had
been trying all along. Couldn't he kid God just this
once? If God wouldn't leave him alone, then he'd keep
going round and round the circle, and tire God out.
'I'm sorry,' he cried. 'I didn't mean to. Moses, stop the
locusts, and I'll turn over a new leaf. Give me back
my business and I'll be a real Christian. Let my wife
get better, and I'll be a true disciple. . . .' I'm sorry,
Pharaoh, but I seem to have mixed you up with all
the Pharaohs who have followed you, and are still
following you.

But Pharaoh, God isn't going to get tired. He will
be patient, and keep following you, until you know
that even to try and run away in the little circles of
your own escaping, is not enough. And Pharaoh is now
very, very near to learning this last lesson of all. That
escape is as impossible as making terms.

The end is in sight. The circles are closing in, and
escape is becoming less and less possible. The last turn
is about to be taken up.

God plunged the land of Egypt into darkness, 'darkness that could be felt'. I don't know what mechanism
God used. But I do know that, for Pharaoh, it was the
right one. To one of his temperament, unannounced,
unwarned, this proved the final word. This is the blackness of a heart that sees the last flickering glimmer of
light and hope disappearing for ever; and doesn't want
the light back, but can hardly let it go.

'Moses,' Pharaoh called; 'what is this? What does this
mean? Moses, can't you do something for me? Is this
the end?'

Moses is silent. There is nothing he can do. It is between God and Pharaoh.

'Then Moses, can't we still make terms?' (The circle is very tight, isn't it, Pharaoh? You are closing in on yourself now, for ever.) 'Moses, what about you going with your children, and just leaving your flocks and herds?'

How patient God has always been. It is this endless patience in Love that has always baffled man. 'Pharaoh, we will go; our children will go; our herds will go; everything about us will go. Not a hoof will remain.'

And now Pharaoh sees, and sees it all. There are no terms. There is no escape. It is God alone, or Pharaoh alone. And Pharaoh now knows all that a rebel man is allowed to know. 'Go away,' he screams. 'Get out of my sight. If ever I see you again, I'll kill you.'

'Yes,' said God. 'You'll never see Me again.' And Pharaoh never saw God again. God saw Pharaoh, of course. He saw the king lose his eldest son, that terribly precious son in the royal household. He saw Pharaoh drive the Hebrews out of Egypt, saw him chase after them, saw him dying in the waters of the sea of reeds as they closed in over his sinking chariot. Yes, God saw all that. He knew all that before Pharaoh, or Egypt, or even this world was here. But Pharaoh didn't see God again.

And that choice, made so finally and so clearly, still stands, alongside the choice of all the Pharaohs of human history. That is the one thing about Pharaoh that does stand. He is gone—his body, with its hormones and central nervous system and cardiovascular system and all the rest of his machinery, has gone. But that choice, that decision, stands and must stand. In some deep sense, that is the tiny, but always-real, scar which God Himself must preserve for ever, to show that the good He has made has been made against real evil. That God is always to be known as the One 'who made light to shine out of darkness', as St. Paul describes this mystic truth.

If you can read this story unmoved, can ponder its

misery and reflect on its enormous implications, without being distressed and disturbed, then you can hardly be man at all. The responsibility of it all, both to Pharaoh as the creature, and to God as the Creator, leaves us with minds reeling and hearts pounding.

And if you saw only that, you could never understand. You would only ever in Pharaoh see one side of the picture—learn one part of the truth. But from Pharaoh you do see one side of the picture—you do learn one part of the truth.

CHAPTER THREE

A SUCCESSFUL CASE

ONE of the Bible doctrines which is very strongly held and taught by the writers of both the Old Testament and the New Testament, but one which is very seldom preached and explained in pulpits and Bible studies, is the doctrine of revelation.

Now I can imagine some of you saying: 'Ah! Here we go—the sixth toe of the third beast; the four horsemen of the Apocalypse; lakes of fire and dragons and all that sort of stuff. Is this Hercus fellow "pre-millennial", "post-millennial" or "a-millennial"? Does he make the book of Revelation agree with the book of Daniel? Is Khruschev the anti-Christ, as lots of cranks have speculated and guessed about Hitler and Mussolini, the Kaiser, Napoleon (and perhaps, even, from across the Rhine, about Churchill and Roosevelt, Lloyd George and Wellington)? This is where we shut this book and read fiction à la Agatha Christie and the genuine novelists.'

But please wait just a minute. That is not the doctrine of revelation, any more than a blood count is the whole story of anaemia. The doctrine of revelation is the simple truth, stated in its simplest form by St. Paul, that 'God has clearly revealed Himself to all men'. Perhaps I now hear you murmuring, 'Yes, much the same really—St. Paul seeing flashing lights and hearing voices on the road to Damascus! Amos seeing plumblines in the hands of God, standing on a wall! All that Psycho-stuff, Trappist monks and Maria Theresa is not my line. I'm a student of economics. . . . And I'm a tool-maker . . . And I'm a school-teacher. . . . And I'm a housewife with three kids and the only dreams and visions I get are just indigestion and a ninety-hour working week.' But again may I stop you, to tell you that this is not the idea at all. This doctrine is the most down-to-earth, practical, everyday truth that

44

man can ever discover. It is the teaching that God has
planned and destined everything you ever encounter,
anywhere in life. And that includes your books and
statistics, Mr. Student; and your lathe and milling
machine, Mr. Tool-maker; and your school appointment and your pupils, Miss School-teacher; and your
three children and your indigestion and your ninety-
hour working week, Mrs. Housewife.

And not only has He planned all this, but He has
done it purposefully, in every detail. He is now using
all these things, and all the other things He has made
in your life (that is the whole of your life, of course),
to effect His heavenly, cosmic will.

Now I must admit quickly that neither you nor I
nor St. Paul nor anyone else, except Jesus Himself, is
really able to appreciate that practically. No-one taught
this truth more clearly than St. Paul; but I would
never for a moment think that, as he sat down to lunch
in the home of host Gaius in Corinth, in his conscious
mind he was aware of the fact that the bit of gristle
he politely swallowed, or the broken lace on his left
sandal—that in all these tiny bits and pieces that really
make up life, he could claim to understand that these
were experiences where God was revealing Himself to
His apostle. No. But St. Paul would also remind us
that the only reason he didn't see it all like that was
because of the smallness of his human mind. He ad-
mitted he could now know only in part, see only as in
a mirror, distorted. But God is not knowing in part,
God is not looking into mirrors. He is the Maker, the
Designer, the Architect. And He is also the Managing
Director of the whole project. (Can you now appreciate
better the wonderment and exultation of St. Paul as he
reminds us that one day we shall know even as we are
known? Can you share the excitement of St. John in
the incredible thought that we shall be like Him, for
we shall see Him as He is: not just in the shadowy
glimpses we perceive in His revelation to us while we
are mere men?)

Then what is it that God is revealing? What does

He want us to see? Surely that is the sixty-four dollar question. And to try to explain that answer to you, I am going to ask you to come back down the pages of history for 2,500 years, and actually to watch the essential process in action, as God Himself has preserved a record of His encounter with one man. There we may together learn the answer to our own lives.

The story of this man is a 'big' story, as befits a 'big' doctrine. In fact the man is himself a giant in history, in many respects, *the* giant. You will not complain that you and I, who are ordinary little men, are therefore excluded from it all. Nor will you suggest that God can reveal Himself only to V.I.P.s and big-shots. Of course not. Rather, surely, you would appreciate that our Lord, who is the Teacher, is true to His role of teaching in taking as a demonstration case one which will be dramatic enough and obvious enough to make the truth crystal-clear. Enough to show us the doctrine so plainly, that it will then be easy for us to scale the experience down to fit the small, humdrum world in which we ourselves are placed.

And so to Nebuchadnezzar, king of Babylon. Nebuchadnezzar, one of the greatest kings in all history; and in many regards, the very greatest.

This is the man who built more brick buildings than any other man has ever done. The man who, by use of his own imagination and power, is the planner and builder of the first city that would be thought really great on modern standards. Fine parks, squares, public places, all laid out in magnificent orderliness. Splendid buildings, the whole city walled by a huge fortified rampart. This is Nebuchadnezzar's Babylon. We are going to look into the story of a man who is an utter despot, a man of violent passions and moods; and yet an intellectual, a savant, a man who loves culture, a man whose city found plenty of space for libraries and learning. This, then, is the man in whose life God will now be seen moving, as He reveals Himself.

The first recorded move that God made was effected even before Nebuchadnezzar came to the throne. He was still only Crown Prince, appointed under his aged, failing father, Nabopolassar, when God stepped into his life. God sent him down to Jerusalem.

'Ho!' you say. 'That's the stuff. Getting him to hear old Jeremiah. Giving him a chance to discuss the philosophical argument for monotheism; or hear some Hebrew pundit expound on the implication of the doctrine of substitutionary atonement in relation to the concepts of comparative religions. That ought to show him.' . . . 'And I wish that Godless colleague of mine would only come and hear our minister.' 'That girl I was talking to in the office, should go and hear Billy Graham.' No, nothing of the kind. Nebuchadnezzar is no more ready to hear Jeremiah than the mechanic in the local garage, or the wife of the village publican, would be ready to read Calvin's *Institutes*. God hasn't the mind of a man. He isn't bound by the obscurantism of the ultra-conservative fundamentalist, any more than He is befogged by the indecisive immaturity of the liberal theologian. He is Light, Truth. He sees clean through the young prince, sees every way of approach. God sent Nebuchadnezzar down to Jerusalem to take captive Jehoiakim, the king.

The tiny Hebrew people in Jerusalem were a turbulent and uncomfortable little kingdom, fretting and plotting rebellion against Babylonian rule. And Nebuchadnezzar took off Jehoiakim and set up Zedekiah in puppet rule, instead. And because God knew every detail of Nebuchadnezzar's personality, he knew that the prince would not just take Jehoiakim and the royal family. God knew that Nebuchadnezzar was not the sort of man who would just crash in and wreck a place. Tyrant and all that he was, he had the mind of a builder; he was an intellectual. And so Nebuchadnezzar did what God wanted him to do. Nebuchadnezzar told his Babylonian officers to cull through the Hebrew people, and pick out all the medically fit, intelligent, skilled young men, who would profit from training and education in the Euphrates metropolis, and so strengthen the already mighty Babylon.

I don't know how their mass surveys were conducted. We like to think that our modern medical screening, I.Q. and Personality Performance Tests and the like, are very new and superior to anything ever done in dark, pre-science ages. But they had their methods, and back to Babylon with the captive king, Jehoiakim, went a small band of top-rating Hebrews. Off to the huge, rapidly developing city, to enter the palace college, to share the king's own fare, to enjoy the learning and education of the great empire capital. To come under the watchful eye of Ashpenaz, the Royal Chamberlain.

It was Ashpenaz who was responsible for the care and health of these prize captives. No stud master ever attended his prize animals more carefully than he watched over the captive students. As he checked their weight, pinched them to make sure they stayed prime plump stock, turned down their eyelids, looked at their tongues, made all the little checks that the science of his age suggested, Ashpenaz was only too well aware that his own life was at stake. Laxity on his part, a loss in the condition of the student stock, and his was the head that would roll. He knew his Nebuchadnezzar.

You may well imagine, then, his concern when one day four of these young men paraded themselves before him with the most outrageous suggestion. These four men were named Daniel, Hananiah, Mishael and Azariah. Daniel was their spokesman. 'Sir,' he said politely; 'we are not used to the royal fare we are getting here. We have grown up on a more vegetable diet, with water to drink; and while we know that our present rich food is entirely suitable for the king and his royal household, we are of much more lowly tastes and background. Do you think that we might, please, revert to our old régime?'

Ashpenaz was as impressed with this gracious and simple request as our society would be if all temperance and similar organizations were to present their arguments in such temperate manner. But he shook his head. 'Gentlemen, I can't risk it. At the next royal inspection, His Highness, who himself drew up your diet charts, would spot it. He has an eye like a hawk. And if the other students of your age group were in better condition than you were, my head would be in danger. I daren't risk it.'

But Daniel and his three friends were not to give up. The steward who tended them in person was their next point of appeal. They knew him better and could talk more freely. 'Look,' said Daniel; 'try it out for ten days. Give us some vegetables to eat, water to drink, and see what happens. Then you watch our complexions and check us over, and decide on what you find out.'

The steward was impressed, and impressed enough. Enough to institute the first controlled clinical trial that I know of, in all the literature of Dietetics and Nutrition. And at the end of the ten days these four men were better in appearance and 'fatter in flesh' than the control group, which consisted of all the fellows who were on the king's rich food. The experiment had succeeded. They were allowed to carry on in their new freedom.

And a well-pleased Ashpenaz now slept soundly, as he knew that at the next royal inspection, the quick eye of the young king, expert stud owner that he was, would be delighted to see the fine condition and appearance of these choice human cattle.

And far more importantly, as they came up to sit for the finals, with Nebuchadnezzar himself conducting their viva voce examinations, these four finished away out on top. In every subject they were far ahead even of the experts in the faculties. Top honours, Firsts, all four of them. And Daniel took off the gold medal in Psychology! ('Visions and Dreams' they used to call it.)

'Nebuchadnezzar'—let us imagine ourselves asking him—'How's life going? What do you think of your prospects? All your plans shaping up well?' And I can imagine Nebuchadnezzar's answer, as he tells us of the big building plans he has under way in the city; of the huge irrigation project over in the eastern part of the state, near the river Kebar; of his hopes of making more capital out of his victory over Pharaoh Necho (this was a victory he had achieved just as his father, Nabopolassar, died). And I think I hear him add: 'My father's death just at that time really brought me some good fortune. Because as I came back from the battle with Necho, I passed through the little Hebrew king-dom of Jerusalem, and now have some of their people working for me. And at the last graduation ceremony, in the Palace University, some of them topped all of the exams. One of them took off the medal in Psy-chology, with the finest pass we have ever had. I simply haven't a man on the staff who could touch this fellow. Belteshazzar, I call him, and mark my words, one day he will hold a research chair at the very least. A most out-standing young fellow. Really a good year all round! I am very pleased with the way things are shaping.'

And we may smile perhaps, and stand somewhat awed as well, as we recognize that all of this is part of the deeply involved plan God has in hand to reveal Him-self to the king.

We are disturbed, too, to think the king doesn't understand all this. Hadn't we better tell him? Couldn't God organize something, say, to get Daniel to talk to him, and tell him all about it? In imagina-tion, we want to burst in on the king, before he gets off to sleep, and in our human impatience exclaim: 'Nebu-chadnezzar! God is after you. God is after all men. "Thou hast made us toward Thyself", a man of God will be saying many centuries after your time. That truth applies as much to you as ever it will to him, or to me. Can't you see that these events in your young life are of His making, not your own? Don't you realize that God is setting the field for some big play which will break right into your life, and put you on the spot before Him?' And Nebuchadnezzar yawns wearily, un-troubled by such disturbing thoughts, and falls asleep on the royal couch, looking forward to the activities of the next day after the refreshment of a good night's

sleep. And as the young crowned head nodded off, off
into the isolation of slumber, where it would seem that
he was safe from interference from God or man, the
big step was taken. God stepped clean into the innermost part of Nebuchadnezzar's being and laid his soul
bare. God made him dream! Yes, just that. Gave him
a dream! No sermon from Daniel. No dramatized
vision from the captive prophet, Ezekiel, working away
over on the irrigation scheme by the Canal at Kebar.
No, just a dream.

Yet not just any old dream. It was a very worrying
dream. And the king, who was well skilled in understanding dreams, who himself conducted the final vivas
in 'Dreams and Visions', you remember—even he was
stumped by it.

As the next day dawned, Nebuchadnezzar called for
the Psychology Faculty. All the Professors, Readers,
Senior Lecturers, etc., gathered into the Royal Presence.

Nebuchadnezzar had not become virtual master of
the whole world at such a young age by being hesitant
or vague. He came straight to the point. 'Gentlemen,'
he said; 'last night I had a dream, which has me very
deeply troubled.'

Their faces brightened. Psychologists and all that
they were, the king was quite a tyrant, and often quite
unpredictable. They were most relieved to find it was
something so much up their alley. 'Your Majesty,' said
the Dean, voicing all their thoughts, 'tell your servants
the dream, and we will show you the interpretation.'
'Listen to me!' the answer was snapped back. 'If you
do not tell me the dream, and also tell me its interpretation, you have my word, I'll have you torn limb
from limb, and your houses laid in ruins.' As the full
significance of this demand and threat struck them, he
turned with a warm smile, and added, 'But if you do
succeed in telling me what the dream was, and what it
means, you will be rewarded by gifts and great honours.'
Then suddenly stern again: 'Come on then, tell me!"

They knew their king, and they knew that they had
heard him correctly. But hope dies hard. 'Yes, Sir. Tell

us the dream, and we will most certainly tell you what it means, Your Majesty.' There was a moment of tense silence; and the dreadful words dropped in deadly judgment from the king's lips. 'Yes, now I see your petty game. You were stalling for time. You are just a bunch of rogues, cheating your way along until the moon enters its next phase, and it will be too late to press the interpretation of the dream. How can I trust you? You're all liars. If you are clever enough to tell me the dream, then I will admit you are to be trusted to give me the right interpretation. You have heard what I demand.'

A babel of panic burst out. 'But Sir, no-one on earth can do that. . . .' 'And no great king in all history has asked such a thing from his advisers. . . .' 'Sir, only the gods could tell you this: and they don't live in the world of flesh and blood. . . .'

'Arioch! Arioch! Take these lying cheats. Take every member of the whole Faculty. Round up the whole bunch and kill the lot.'

Blazing in furious anger, the king stamped out of the conference chamber, as Arioch, the captain of the palace guards, and his men seized the magicians and sorcerers and hounded them off to their death.

I must say that the next bit of the story is real Gilbert and Sullivan stuff. It reads like pure farce. You see, when it was a matter of interviewing the king, and the chance for royal recognition, only the heads of the department had gone along. Daniel wasn't there of course. Young graduates, no matter how brilliant, don't get included in an invitation like that. Can you see the Prof. turning up at such an important conference with a Ph.D. student in tow, with the risk of having the sparkling mind of the young man completely overshadow the senior men? Never! Never! But when it comes to falling heads, administrative purges, and the like, the little men and the boys are there all right. So that we find Daniel, back at his room, working at his thesis on *Dreams and Portents,* all unaware of the drama that had been enacted in the king's conference hall, when in stalked Arioch to snap the handcuffs on him, and lead him off to the tumbrel.

There was a terrific commotion going on, as all the members of the Faculty were being roped in for the slaughter. But Daniel had been through this sort of thing before! And he knew that in all this trouble, God was still in charge. He knew that God is always the Upholding Principle, as St. Paul teaches us. And this confidence gave Daniel a poise and a serenity that pulled Arioch up short. In Daniel there was nothing of the panic and despair of the other students. With discreet words and prudent tone, Daniel quietly asked Arioch what the trouble was all about. 'Could you tell me why the king has decreed such extreme penalty?'

Utterly disarmed by the controlled and self-disciplined young slave, Arioch told him all about it. And after reciting the story of the trouble, the Captain was in the end quite prepared to release Daniel, to let him seek an audience with the king, and straighten it all out. Have you ever noticed how completely wisely God chooses His men and His methods? Think how altogether devastating a man like Daniel would be if he were let loose as a churchwarden in some sleepy little parish church—it would be utterly unfair. But think also how unfair it would be, if God asked the rather dim-witted vicar of the same sleepy little parish church, to call a nation to repentance and faith. God has His Billy Graham. But He also has His ignorant Sunday School teachers, and mixed-up clergy.

And now we begin to see how God had been working all this time on Nebuchadnezzar. At first glance it all looks like politics, and university days, and the gold medal in Psychology. God has been preparing for just this dramatic, exciting moment. The audience with the king is granted. The execution orders are stayed, until Daniel meets the king. D-day for discussions is to be tomorrow.

That night Daniel and his three trusted young friends prayed to God to tell them the dream, and its interpretation.

And their prayer was answered. Daniel learned the dream and its meaning.

'How was this done?' you ask. 'How did Daniel stumble on the dream? Did he hypnotize the king and wheedle it out of him? Is this telepathy? Thought-transference? Extra-sensory-perception?' (This last one sounds much more impressive, even if it is still really just as vague.) I don't know. I'm not told, and I may only guess, just as you may. And I'll tell you my guess, and you can take it or leave it. My guess is that Daniel went off to bed and dreamed the same dream. Now I said I was guessing, and don't quote me as saying anything else. But the reasons for my guess are, firstly, that dreams are, at any rate from my experience, things you can never sit down and reason into existence. In fact, it is the relative absence of any rational mechanism that makes dreams possible. And secondly, we know that God is the Upholding Principle of everything in all existence. He plans and maintains the path of every electron in orbit. And I can readily enough admit that what to us is a vast complex of repressions, sublimations, sleep-mentor, depolarized cellular membranes, and so on, is to God simply the unfolding of an objective and a purpose which was planned in every detail even before there was such a thing as time.

So that whether or not it is true that Daniel learned the dream by dreaming it himself, is not a bit important. But the tremendous truth, expressed by Daniel the following morning, that 'to God belong wisdom and might', is altogether important. And in his wonder and awe, Daniel praised the God of heaven, exclaiming:

> 'He changes times and seasons;
>   he removes kings and sets up kings;
>   he gives wisdom to the wise
>   and knowledge to those who have
>   understanding;
>   he reveals deep and mysterious things;
>   he knows what is in the darkness,
>   and the light dwells with him.'

Aglow with the excitement of the discovery, Daniel
was still self-controlled enough to behave carefully. He
went directly to Arioch, and stated his finding. 'Sir,'
he said, 'you don't need to destroy the wise men of
Babylon. Bring me into the king's conference chamber
—I have already made an appointment for ten o'clock
—and I will give him the interpretation he is waiting
for.'

I am sure Arioch regarded it as a piece of personal
success on his own part. Don't we all like to think that
our good fortune is of our own making? (I once had
a patient who was wildly cock-a-hoop about his own
cleverness in winning the state lottery. He was quite
sure it was because he had used a clever 'system' of his
own devising!) And bursting with self-importance and
looking for the king's approval of his cleverness, Arioch
announced Daniel. 'Your Majesty, I have succeeded.
I have discovered the man you want. One of the exiles
from Jerusalem will make known to you the interpretation you seek. Here he is, Sir! Daniel.'

Nebuchadnezzar looked at Daniel. And I'm sure the
king's face was glowing with delight. This is the fellow
I called Belteshazzar, wearing my gold medal in Psychology! Of course, of course! Why didn't I think of
it earlier? This fellow is the brightest student we've
ever had in this school. He must have been doing some
wonderful research to get so far ahead of all the rest
of the Faculty. The king looked at Daniel, and his
excitement mounted as he asked the rhetorical question: he knew the answer, but it would be great to
hear the fellow actually give it. 'So your researches have
led you to discover both what the dream was, and
what it means?' 'No, Sir.'

You know that feeling you have, when you're racing
up the stairs, and tread on the top stair that isn't there?
Have you ever been peacefully strolling through the
garden, thinking lovely thoughts, when you stepped on
the head of the rake? Have you ever found yourself in
a strange dark room, peering for the light switch, and
give a whoop of delight as you throw out your hand to

turn it on when you think you see it—and learn only
then that it was only an empty light-socket, and that
some dim-wit had left the power on? Nebuchadnezzar
felt like all these, and all the other things like these, in
that moment.

'No, Sir. No psychologist can possibly do that. But
there is a God in heaven who does reveal mysteries, and
He has made known to you, Sir, in your dream, your
future history. The dream you had was a dream of the
future; and God, who reveals mysteries, has told you
what is yet to be. And He has shown this to me, Your
Majesty, so that I can explain the meaning to you.'
Daniel paused respectfully. He was only a slave and
this was King Nebuchadnezzar, king of all Babylon.

But the king's quick mind was seeing the answer.
'Of course,' he was saying to himself. 'I must find out
how this fellow got the information. I knew when I
conducted that viva that he was a winner. He's easily
the brightest man in the whole Faculty, and I should
have expected this.'

'But Sir,' Daniel broke in on the silence; 'I can't do
this because I am cleverer than the Heads of the Psychology Department. It has nothing to do with being
clever at all.' Then before the king could interrupt, and
start debating and arguing this (Question for Speculation and Academic Discussion: 'Was Nebuchadnezzar
at this point of his philosophical immaturity a Logical
Positivist?'), Daniel plunged straight into the main
subject matter.

'Sir, in your dreams you saw a great image. It was
huge, dazzlingly bright, terrifying. Its head was of pure
gold. Arms and chests of silver. Trunk and thighs of
bronze. Its legs were of iron, and its feet were part iron
and part porcelain. Then as you were watching, a
stone, one that had not been cut in a quarry, struck the
image on its feet of iron and porcelain, and smashed
them to pieces. And then the whole image came crash-
ing down, and the iron and the china and the other
metals were ground to dust. And the wind blew the
whole lot away until there wasn't the tiniest trace of it

all left. And then, as you watched, the stone that had broken the image began to get bigger and bigger, until it became a huge mountain, and finally filled the whole earth.'

Daniel paused again. He had no need to ask the king if it was the right dream. The young man who as Crown Prince had largely helped his father wipe out the Assyrian capital of Nineveh, the one who had routed Pharaoh Necho, the king who at this very moment was engaged in the greatest construction programme ever planned in a single lifetime—this man was sitting there with beads of perspiration on his forehead, his pupils dilated with fear and excitement, his hands gripping fiercely to the arms of the royal throne, as he relived the awful dream that had been haunting him ever since that night he first dreamed it. Yes. Daniel knew it was the right dream. He knew God doesn't make mistakes. And with the same quiet confidence, he plunged right into the explanation.

'That, then, was the dream, Sir. Now I will tell you what it means. You, Sir, are the king of all kings alive. The God of heaven has given to you all the honour and glory and power there is in the world. And He has made you ruler over every man and beast there is. You, Sir, are the head of gold. After your reign you will be followed by a less kingly king. Then in turn, a third kingdom, but only of bronze, Sir, will cover the world. Then a fourth, strong, hard as iron, which will crush everything else it meets. But as you saw, the feet made partly of iron and partly of porcelain, point to a divided strength, with the hardness of iron, but the brittleness of china. And then the God of heaven will set up a kingdom which will never be broken. And it will entirely wipe out all these other kingdoms. And as you noticed very particularly, in your dream, that the image was broken by a stone which had not been quarried by human hands, the interpretation clearly shows that the great God of heaven has told you what He will do, and how His own kingdom will end all other kingdoms, and it will stand for ever. Sir, the dream is a true portent of future events, and that is its true meaning.'

The king's face was simply alight with excitement. As Daniel finished speaking, standing quietly to attention, Nebuchadnezzar leapt out of his chair, and actually prostrated himself at the young student's feet. Gone altogether the fear, the awe, the tension and the depression of the dream. Now a near manic state of delight and approval gripped the king.

'Guards! Priests!' he shouted wildly. 'Come on. We must celebrate this wonderful moment. Put on the ceremonial offering. And plenty of incense. This is terrific.' Then turning back excitedly to Daniel: 'My goodness, your God is an absolutely super God. Your God must be a wizard. Fancy a God who can tell dreams! You have certainly cleaned this one up.'

And then and there, as the ceremonial honours for Daniel were being enacted, Nebuchadnezzar was carried away by it all. No mere victory in battle was to him as wonderful as this. Designing and building his huge city, with its great forts and roof gardens, was to him better satisfaction than just winning battles—but this! Why, this is the most enthralling thing he has ever struck. A god that can reveal dreams! 'Daniel,' he burst out, 'I will make you a rich man. I'll give you a knighthood. No. An earldom. By heavens, man, I'll make you a duke, and not a penny less. Duke it is, and you will be chief ruler over the whole of the city of Babylon, and you can take over my own post of Chancellor of the University.'

And in this half-fairy-tale, half-Gilbert-and-Sullivan piece of real-life history, Daniel kept his head. What a man! He knew full well, that in all this sudden and tremendous change of plans, with all the pressure on his time that the new duties and privileges would bring, he would be in grave spiritual danger. Quick as lightning he saw the answer—the answer that would keep for him the spiritual strength of some measure of real fellowship, the opportunity for prayer and study of God's word and will. 'Thank you very much, Your

Majesty. And you may be assured, Sir, that I will do all in my power to help you and serve you well. But, Sir, I have three companions, all very able men indeed, who are also servants of the same God of heaven. It would be a very great strength to me, and to your cause, if they could share the work with me.'

And lo and behold, wonders will never cease. Shadrach, Meshach and Abednego, which are the Babylonian names for Mishael, Hananiah and Azariah, are appointed governors of the provinces surrounding the city, while Daniel remains ruler in Babylon itself.

'Nebuchadnezzar, how's tricks? Everything still shaping up nicely? Got any difficulties you can't puzzle out? Any real worries?' Nebuchadnezzar grins cheerfully. 'Wonderful!' he exclaims. 'Am I just the lucky, lucky dog! You remember that Hebrew slave I told you about? The one that set the record pass in Dreams and Visions? Am I lucky and glad to have found him! You would never believe this, but he has a God who can actually tell him what other people have dreamed! Just think of it. And not only that, but this God also tells the fellow what the dream means! This must be about the most wonderful man you can have in a place of responsibility. He is as reliable as the rising of the sun, and I've made him ruler over the whole great city. And three of his companions worship the same God, and they are now Governors of the surrounding provinces. I'm just the luckiest man. . . .' And his voice dies away, as he walks off to superintend some vital matter of planning and state. . . .

While I seem to hear in his place the subdued babel of all the other Nebuchadnezzars, great and small, of other years and this year, as they say the same thing: 'Of course, I don't go to Church myself, you know, but it's a jolly fine thing to see our lovely Queen taking such an active place in Church affairs. We could do with a bit more religion, don't you think? . . .' 'We send ours to the Methodist Sunday School. It's very close to our home and we think our children should have every advantage. . . .' 'Is there anything else,

General?' 'Why, of course, Colonel. Make a note to
Corps Headquarters to be more insistent on regular
Church parades. Too many exercises have been allowed
to break in on them. We must keep up the men's
morale at highest pitch, and religion is the best thing
in the world to help that.'

Yes, Nebuchadnezzar, you have learnt something;
something that puts you in the company of a great
many people in this world. You have learnt that God
is quite a force to be reckoned with; that God is a valuable addition to your list of useful things in life. And
even though you still think that God is an 'it', a 'thing',
a 'technique' for learning, for understanding dreams,
you have at least learnt that. You have still the mind of
a materialist, but your materialist mind has been given
a bias that will for ever separate you from the confused
group of Logical Positivists and Realists and the like.
You will finally come to discover that the God you
thought was a useful psychological technique is in fact
the One who rolls every star in its heavenly path; and
that He is the One who, working in the myriad intrica-
cies of a human cerebral cortex, gave you that disturbing dream.

And so God has moved in. He has moved in in the
person of Daniel, governor of the city of Babylon; and
of Shadrach, Meshach and Abednego, governors of the
provinces. And it is these three provincial governors
who provide the next spiritual jumping-off point.

Nebuchadnezzar was probably no more a megalo-
maniac than almost any simple man. But he had so
much social scope and equipment that his megalo-
manic expressions are very much more clearly expressed. I am guessing a bit in the story here, but I
think my guess is correct enough. I think that Nebuchadnezzar was ordinary enough to want to be noticed
and approved. But having been provided by society
with despotic powers of sheer fairy-tale greatness, he
proceeded to take appropriate, but quite extraordinary,
steps to make certain that he was in *fact* noticed and

approved. In the city this was easy enough. It was just
a matter of a Royal Parade, no doubt with Daniel riding along respectfully at his side. And Nebuchadnezzar
could see with his own sharp enough eyes, that every
Tom, Dick and Harry fell flat on his face before him.
Yes, that was easy, and it was great fun. But in the
provinces it was harder. He couldn't get out there often
enough; also it was a bit difficult to superintend. After
all, it's no satisfaction to sit at home, and just think
and hope that you are liked and approved. Far better
to do it all out in the open, publicly, and make sure.
At any rate this is my guess as to how and why Nebuchadnezzar did what he did do next.

He had his workmen make a great gold image, nearly
a hundred feet high, probably carved in wood, but entirely overlaid with gold, and erect it out in the provincial plains. And there he had a ceremonial parade
organized, so that at the appropriate moment, as the
band played the national anthem, or fanfare, or whatever it was, everyone took that as the cue to fall flat,
and so acknowledge allegiance to the king.

When I was a small schoolboy we had, in the school
I attended, a weekly ceremony which was called 'Saluting the Flag'. Now we also had as our reigning king at
that time King George V. In those boyhood days, I had
always had for King George V the affection that probably I would have felt for my grandfathers had they
been alive. But to stand out on a bare tarred pavement,
where the tar melted and stuck to our feet in summer,
and where the puddles were covered with a thin crust
of ice in winter, and there salute the flag, certainly did
nothing to add to my affection for the king. Fortu-
nately, I never once associated King George with the
whole thing. I regarded it as part of the preparation for
war, and an introduction to soldiering, and therefore
quite properly unpleasant. Yet, looking back, I can see
that our 'Saluting the Flag' ceremony, and the ceremony that Nebuchadnezzar was planning out in the
fields of the provinces of Babylon, are alike. Yet Nebuchadnezzar had far too good a brain to let his ceremony

degenerate into something trite and ordinary, like that.
Not a bit of it.

For alongside the huge, golden image, Nebuchadnezzar ordered that there should be built a great furnace. And as the ceremony was put under way, the
decree went forth to the assembled multitude, that anyone who refused to salute and worship the image would
be tossed into this blazing furnace. The huge licking
tongues of flame, and the billowing clouds of jet black
smoke from the burning bitumen, with the glinting
flash of the golden image, must have been one of the
most stirring and impressive tableaux ever devised. It
only needed some foolhardy reactionary to refuse to
make the salute, to provide the drama to end all
dramas.

And this was exactly what happened. It happened
almost before the thing was fully organized. It was at
the Dedication Ceremony, when the audience was entirely composed of V.I.P.s, that Shadrach, Meshach and
Abednego did just that! They refused to salute the
image! The decree was read, the band struck up, and
all the satraps, prefects, governors, counsellors, trea-
surers, justices, magistrates and officials fell flat on their
faces. And these three stood glaringly, recklessly, un-
ashamedly upright! And these three were the three provincial governors, the pets of the king.

What a scene! And what a chance for the disgruntled,
jealous Chaldean governors whom they had displaced.

It seems that Nebuchadnezzar was not himself present
at this Dedication Ceremony. I like to think that he
was just the tiniest bit self-conscious; embarrassed ever
so slightly at this bit of blatant self-advertising. And so
he did not see this Terrible Thing. But he soon heard
all about it. The Chaldeans collected up a small depu-
tation, and hot-footed it to His Majesty.

'Sir,' said the spokesman. 'There seems to be some
slight confusion concerning this saluting ceremony with
the golden image. We understand that when the music
breaks out from the band, everyone within earshot
should fall down and worship the image, under penalty

of being hurled into the blazing furnace.' He paused just that dramatic moment, to watch the fire light in the king's eye, to see the tightening of the line of the royal lips. 'But, Sir, there are three Jews, Shadrach, Meshach and Abednego, whom you appointed as provincial governors, who do not pay the slightest heed to your decree at all. They blatantly spurn your gods and your image.'

Nebuchadnezzar was livid with rage. He raced to his chariot and whipped his way out to the parade ground where the image and the furnace were standing. 'Bring the three men to me,' he shouted. Shadrach, Meshach and Abednego stood in front of him, all dressed in their robes of office. (And perhaps all wearing their hoods from the University of Babylon.) Nebuchadnezzar's face softened. These were the three brilliant colleagues of Daniel. These three were all worshippers of the God of heaven, the dream-telling God. They're foreigners, and perhaps not entirely up on the more cultured ethos of Babylon. That must be it. They haven't quite understood the business. 'Gentlemen,' he said. 'I understand that you did not worship my gods, and the golden image which I have had set up. Now when you are ready, we will have the band play the fanfare again, and then if you fall down and worship the image, which I have made, we will consider the episode closed.' It was really a gracious speech, and for such a tyrant and despot, singularly forgiving. But as he said it, something in the manner, something in the poise of these three men, struck him. He paused a moment, then thundered out: 'But if you don't worship, you will be pitched into the blazing fiery furnace.' And then the hurt pride, and the insecurity that is always the measure of the man, flared up in him. 'And I'd like to see the God that can deliver you out of my clutches then!'

The three Hebrews stood still. Their hearts were pounding, the sweat stood out on their foreheads, but their answer told just what their real values were. 'Sir,' they said; 'we can give you our answer straight out. Our God, whom we serve, is quite well able, if He wills it, to deliver us out of the blazing furnace, and out of your hand too, Your Majesty. But whether He does in fact deliver us or not, we serve Him and we will not serve your gods or your image.'

The blood drained out of Nebuchadnezzar's face, as he listened to this death challenge. There was something in the strong confidence of the three men, even in their fear and danger, that almost unnerved him. He had sneered at their God, the dream-telling God, and they had calmly accepted the challenge on behalf of their God, and were defying him to his face.

The initial shock was burned up in an overwhelming fury. This was no longer a God who provided helpful formulae—a God who was a sort of extra subject which was a useful supplement to Algebra and Economics and Psychology. This was a God who interfered in people's lives, and could make a nuisance of Himself. The orders were barked out as the circulating adrenalin parched his throat and dried his lips. The pulse pounding in his ears matched the passion thundering in his mind: 'Make the furnace hotter! Twice as hot! . . . Hotter still. . . . Seven times as hot. Generals! Brigadiers! Line up in front. Take them. Tie them up in their robes, their hats, every single rag they've got. Get a move on. Now into the furnace with them.'

Nebuchadnezzar was still quite a young man, but he had been an active campaigner since his youth. Yet the generals and top-brass had never seen him as furious as this. Those tremendous earlier days when, with his old father, Nabopolassar, the young Crown Prince had wiped out Nineveh; those few exciting days when, on the plains of Megiddo, he had routed Pharaoh Necho. All of these, and other such occasions, had never provided a fury and rage like this. Of course not. Man at war with man is never quite like man at war with God. (Unless he sees that the one is in fact the other.)

And the firemen were in a state of near panic as they poured on more and yet more fuel into the searing furnace. And the brass-hats were a-tremble as they bound the three Jews and rushed them into the furnace. Into

the furnace that was now an uncontrollable abyss of
flame. Flame that rolled and leapt, and suddenly aval-
anched out upon the generals and their prisoners and
swallowed them all up in a great engulfing roar of red-
black death.

Nebuchadnezzar froze in astonishment and awe at
this sudden deadly blow. He leapt out of the chair he
had been seated on, standing on tiptoe—half hoping
his eyes and ears had deceived him, half hoping it was
indeed true—the terrible lurch as the generals' knees
and strength gave way to hurl them face-forward into
the inferno; the sudden piercing screams of fear that
had come from the throats of the doomed men. These
things his eyes and ears had told him. Yet was there
perhaps that fraction-of-a-second whimsy that will at
such a time intrude even into the most serious and
tragic setting—the whimsy that now he has lost a lot
of his top-brass he can do all those reshuffling of commands that he has been wanting to do for years now,
and that in army-life of all ages, are so hard to come
by? These old soldiers so often neither die nor fade
away.

I don't know. I don't know if Nebuchadnezzar even
had that same trouble in his army. But I do know this:
I know that he had that curious mixture of elation and
terror that takes a man whenever he pits his little might
against God, that soaring moment when he has shaken
his fist at God, and claimed victory; and the sick hollow
feeling in the pit of the stomach as he knows all at the
same time that God is just waiting His own time to
strike back.

Yes. Nebuchadnezzar felt all that as, with tight-
caught breath and staring eyes, he peered into the furnace. And his breath could not come, nor could he cease
from staring, as his eyes saw something even more
frightening than that terrible dream that had first
brought these men into office. And now this was no
dream. This was men being incinerated in a roaring
furnace. Yet this was an even more terrible nightmare,
for the men were moving around in the middle of the

fire. Yes, they were. It was not a trick of his imagination. It was not just an eerie phantasm in the rolling
smoke and flames. It was the three men he had sen-
tenced to death and there they were alive in the middle
of this fiery vortex! And as he saw them he knew—no
need to ask, to speculate, to philosophize. The awful
truth stunned him. Their God had done it. He had
saved them, kept them alive, even in the middle of this
terrible flame. This dream-telling technique was in
fact a furnace-delivering God! This God had taken up
the challenge and had saved His worshippers!

And as these and such thoughts flashed through his
mind the king reeled as if struck by a blow between
the eyes. For there, in the furnace, with the three provincial governors, was their God Himself. Oh no! Not
that. Please not a God who comes and gets right alongside people! Please not a God who saves men, by coming and joining men in their trial!

Nebuchadnezzar jumped up, and raced to the nearest
of his now terrified advisers. 'Didn't we throw three
men into the fire?'

How hardly man gives in to God! If it is true that
any fool can ask a question, then surely this was a question even unworthy of a fool. Surely the King of all
Babylon could count Shadrach, Meshach and Abednego, one, two, three!

But the counsellors are too anxious, too upset, much
too fearful to answer more than a quick 'Yes, Sir.' 'But
I can see four men, loose, walking around in the fire!'
is the king's agonized exclamation, 'and the fourth one
looks like a son of the gods!'

Barely able to breathe, caught up in the pathos of
the disturbance of this terrible truth, Nebuchadnezzar
walked over to the door of the furnace. Indeed, I think
it would probably be more fair to say that while Nebuchadnezzar was wrestling in his mind with the awesome
stirring of his imagination, his legs and feet just carried
him over to the furnace. And a voice that was his, yet
not his, called 'Shadrach, Meshach, Abednego! Servants
of the Most High God. Come out. Come here.' And out

they came, alone; just the three men. No God with them. Just Shadrach, Meshach, Abednego.

What a moment. What a scene. What a buzz and a sizzle and a twitter of a babel of astonishment as the satraps and the prefects and the governors and the other officials all gathered and fussed and fingered and sniffed and chattered. 'Not a mark on them.' 'Not a single singed eyebrow, even.' 'By all the gods, old chap, I swear I sniffed all round 'em like a jolly old retriever, what! And not even the merest soupçon of the smell of fire on one of them. Just wait till I get back to the "Kemosh Arms" and tell all the fellows.'

Yes, you could fill in all the bits you like—the gossip and the questions and the explanation and all the rest of it. I've often puzzled over it myself. Let me admit that the little bit of thermo-dynamics that ever I learnt, with its adiabatics and isothermals, Carnot cycles and Entropy, I found singularly dull—until I stopped to think and marvel at this story. And then I wished I knew all the thermo-dynamics in the world, to understand the air currents, vortices, the combustion-chemistry, the . . . and I bow my head, humbled, as I see that it is not all the thermo-dynamics in the world, it is all the thermo-dynamics in heaven, that I need to know— to know as God does the trajectory of every electron in orbit, the kinetic exchange of every molecule in existence, to plan and direct a wonder such as this. This is real miracle. This is where, as man, a creature with about thirteen hundred and fifty grams of brain, I see the Creator, God, at work. Where I see the unfathomable greatness of the Mind to whom all things are known.

And in humility of heart, and bowed low in wondering awe, I turn again to watch Nebuchadnezzar. He is still standing there, clasping the hand of first one, and then another, of his three governors. There is no longer the terror, the panic of those few awful earlier minutes. But neither is there quite the same expression that was on his face yesterday. Or the day before that, or any day before at all. There is now the manner and maturity that belongs to those who have seen God actually working in the experiences of other men. Imagination has now a new, a further horizon. Wonder has a greater depth. All emotion has a deeper expression. Nebuchadnezzar has this look. It's new, it's impressive, it suits him.

He is saying something—let us push up closer and hear what it is. He is talking to his counsellors now. Listen—'Full marks to the God of Shadrach, Meshach and Abednego. These fellows trusted Him. They completely disregarded my commands, and even sacrificed their lives, rather than worship any other God. And their God sent His angel and saved them.'

But watch. He's jumping up on his throne. He's standing on it. He's holding up his hand for silence. He's going to say something important. Here it comes ... 'Therefore I make this decree: any people or nation or language that says anything against the God of Shadrach, Meshach and Abednego shall be torn limb from limb, and their houses laid in ruins. There is no other God who can deliver like this.'

Yes, Nebuchadnezzar, there is no other God who can deliver like this. In fact, there is no other God at all. All the other gods are just reflections (all too often just distorted reflections) of Him. You are right, Nebuchadnezzar. Very right. This God is a God to be served. He is not an 'It', even if you give the impersonal pronoun a capital 'I'. He is 'He', personal pronoun, capital 'H'. Nebuchadnezzar, you have joined the group of great men (and this is what makes them great, of course, not thrones or cash or brains) who have stood in the same awe and felt the same stirring of reverence, as they have seen Him concerned in the lives of their fellow-men.

Fathers have sometimes seen it in their sons; sons in their fathers. Historians have at times seen it in the pages of history. Poets have at times seen it in nature, in war, in the love of a man for a maid. Nebuchadnezzar, I and my fellow-doctors, perhaps more than any other men alive, see this. As we watch men and women going down into the valley of the shadow, there come just now and again those humbling occasions, when we see the sufferer supported by his God, who seems to be standing alongside the sick bed, giving strength and support that no doctor ever hopes to match. This is the thing which must at times make our antibiotics and steroids and polysynaptic blocking agents lose their title of 'Wonder Drug', and be seen as the mere technological developments that they really are.

Nebuchadnezzar, almost half the world saw this a few years ago, and that time in the experience of a king, too. We saw a monarch dying ahead of his time, looking back on days of grave trouble, and looking ahead into times of even less real hope and calmly saying:

'I said to the man who stood at the Gate of the Year, "Give me a light whereby I may venture into the unknown." And he said unto me, "Put your hand into the Hand of God, which is better than a light, and safer than a known way." '

Nebuchadnezzar, nearly all the world saw it again, later still, in the radiant experience of the daughter of that same king, as she then assumed her late father's throne. As she accepted the office of Queen, as she vowed her holy vows, as she dedicated herself to her duty, we saw (and who on earth did not have eyes to see this?) that her hand was in the hand of God too, that all the loveliness that made her woman was but part of the far greater glory that was hers because she, like her father before her, like Shadrach, Meshach and Abednego before him, was a servant of the Most High God.

Nebuchadnezzar, it's back to work again, back to war again, back to the rich world of planning and building, to all the tasks and pleasures that belong to the life of the king of Babylon the Great. But Nebuchadnezzar, you will never again be the same as you were yesterday. Something has happened to you that moved you a full step nearer your end. It wasn't that you met God. You weren't ready for that. But you saw three other men do

it, live it. And while their God did not step out of the
fire and claim you too, it was only because He is a God
of great compassion and longsuffering. He is biding
His time, not yours.

Nebuchadnezzar, while you may be quickly forgetting that drama of the day you saw God walking alongside three of His men, in the furnace of your making,
God is certainly not forgetting.

Oh yes, you have given Him your official approval,
we know. But your approval means nothing to God.
It might simplify things for Shadrach, Meshach and
Abednego. It might make it just a tiny bit easier for
poor Ezekiel, as he has to dumb-act his prophecies over
in the slave-labour camp, digging canals at Kebar. But
God is not seeking or needing your approval. Oh yes,
Nebuchadnezzar, God gets quite a lot of approval.
There is never a Christmas, a Good Friday, or Easter
Day without a spate of editorials in all the leading
papers in the land pouring out quite lavish approval
on God and His affairs. Nebuchadnezzar, if God were
to advertise in the *Sydney Morning Herald* that He
had need of patrons, we would need to put on extra
sorters at the Post Office to handle the mail. Indeed
Sir, if you press us hard, we will have to admit that
almost all the buildings, stained-glass windows, schools,
hospitals, pipe-organs and the rest of things that the
Church owns all over the world, have to an embarrassingly large extent been financed by our patrons.

And now, Nebuchadnezzar, God is going to leave
you for several years, as you think this over. He doesn't
always do that. In fact, He doesn't often do that. But
you can think—He has made you an intellectual. As
you near the completion of your main city building
projects, God will leave you thinking, and thinking.
And when next He clearly shows His hand in your life,
it will not be with Him in the fiery furnace and you
outside. Not a bit of it. It will be in that face-to-face
meeting, that I-to-Thou encounter, that first-person
singular to second-person singular relationship which
will for ever determine your destiny.

And in my imagination I seem to hear the heavenly gong being sounded for this third and last round —God is in the ring with Nebuchadnezzar and this time it is for the K.O. Man always interprets the approach of God as a threat to his very life (which in one sense, of course, it is). And yet, because God is love, He will make it the kindest possible K.O. And also because He is love, He cannot be true to Himself and baulk at delivering the blow.

And God sent Nebuchadnezzar reeling across the ring, with a blow where Nebuchadnezzar would feel it—would feel it most. A solid right to the head. God gave him another dream!

There is in the story of God and Nebuchadnezzar something that stirs and thrills me through and through. Yet perhaps nothing more than this very move. I am a very ordinary sort of fellow, and don't dream very much at all. Indeed, any dream I do have is a shadowy, unconvincing jumble, which I could never hope to untangle and make sense out of. I think that if I had a nice interesting dream, like this one God gave to Nebuchadnezzar, I would probably be so confoundedly conceited about it, that it would only make me feel rather smug.

But Nebuchadnezzar was a very different man indeed. He was a man to whom dreams conveyed all sorts of portents and omens. To him a dream was not a mere caricatured externalization of the unconscious mind. Not a bit of it—it was really serious business. So serious, that it sent him into a flat spin! He was in a panic! Terrified! He called in the experts to advise him about his dream, and they could not help him either. Daniel was not among them, of course. He had moved right out of this academic world of professors and lecturers, into the big world of city-governor. But Nebuchadnezzar, in his dire distress with his dream, remembered Daniel's gold medal in Psychology; remembered most vividly the dream of the great image; remembered, no doubt at all, the way the God of dreams had been discovered to be the God of

the men of the fiery furnace. And he sent post-haste for
Daniel.

Daniel had hardly come through the door before the
king started to pour out his tale. 'Daniel, another
dream. It has me worried to death. I am really
frightened. You listen to it, and see if you can help
me. You're easily the greatest expert that we have on
dreams, and I know you have a true personal faith in
the God of dreams. You must help me. Listen: in my
dream, I saw a tree growing out in a field. It was a
splendid big tree and it kept growing and growing
until it seemed to grow right up into the heavens. And
you could see it from anywhere in the world. It was a
most beautiful tree to look at, and it produced an
abundant fruit crop—enough to feed the whole world.
All the animals found shade under it; all the birds
nested in it; and it was a source of food for all.

'And then in my dream, I saw a heavenly Watcher
coming down out of the skies. And he called out,
"Chop the tree down. Cut off its branches. Tear off all
its leaves and throw away all of its fruit. Chase away
all the animals from under it, and shoo off all the
birds nesting in it. But leave the stump of the tree to
stand in the ground, and bind the stump with a brass
and iron band. Leave the bound stump standing in the
lush tender grass of the field."'

He paused, and the reaction of fear, that Daniel had
seen the first time they ever met like this, was halting
his speech. The memory and the concern at a sudden
change of imagery in language, in the pronoun, of the
dream account, made Nebuchadnezzar feel quite sick
with anxiety. 'Daniel!' he burst out, as he passed his
tongue over his fear-parched lips. 'Listen now to this.
He said, "Let him be wet with the dew of heaven. Let
him live with the beasts out in the grass. Let his mind
be changed from a man's, and let a beast's mind be
given to him, and allow seven seasons to pass."'

Nebuchadnezzar moved forward on to the edge of
his chair, and went on now in a half-whisper. 'Daniel,
then He said (and this is word for word) "The sentence

is by the decree of the Watchers. The decision is by the word of the Holy ones, in order that the living may know that the Most High rules the kingdom of men: that He gives it to whom He will, and He sets over it the lowliest of men." Daniel, I swear I saw all of that. I heard every word of it. None of the University staff in Babylon can help me, but I know you can. Daniel, the spirit of the Holy God is in you, and you can tell me what it means. Do please help me. I know you can.'

Surely you must be moved, as you see the pathos of this great king so greatly humbled. Here he is in the ring with God, beaten to his knees with this remarkably simple, but effective, blow. And pleading desperately for help from Daniel—help from Daniel, because in his innermost thoughts he was becoming aware that God was somehow getting out of the fiery furnace at last, and getting into his dreams—and Daniel was one of God's men, and his only hope of escape was help like this.

Whether you find this heart-moving or not is your own business. But I confess I find it so. And so did Daniel. He sat there as still as death, chin cupped in his hand, as the dream was told. And as he began to piece together the information the dream was conveying, his face fell into an expression of gloom and alarm. He sat there staring fixedly into space, unanswering. It was Nebuchadnezzar who pulled him out of his reverie. 'Daniel!' he finally called out. 'Tell me what you know. Don't be afraid to tell me the truth about the dream and its meaning. I simply must know the truth.'

Daniel was swallowing hard at a big lump in his throat that seemed to choke him; he was blinking away tears that he could not wish to hide. He and Nebuchadnezzar were friends in the pattern of friendship two great men may share when each so warmly respects the capacity of the other. 'Sir!' he burst out, 'this dream would only ever please someone who hated you! Only your bitterest enemies would like the interpretation of it.'

He turned and faced the king, more composed after this outburst, sure of himself as he could recognize his place in the whole episode, seeing himself as the angel of God, sent to teach and warn Nebuchadnezzar.

'The lovely tree you saw, Your Majesty, growing larger and larger, and providing food and shelter to the whole world—it is you. You have become great and strong. Now your dominion extends virtually to the furthest corner of the earth. And whereas you saw the heavenly Watcher command the tree to be chopped down, it means, Sir, that the Most High has decreed that you will be driven out of your place among men. He has decided to cause you to live like a wild animal for seven seasons, and also until you come to learn that it is God who really rules in human kingdoms and that it is He who gives it to any man He chooses.'

Nebuchadnezzar was hardly breathing as this simple and terrible dream was declared. But before he could reply, Daniel went on, 'And as you heard the command to leave the stump in the ground, God has decreed that your kingdom will not be taken from you permanently, but He will restore it to you as soon as you come to admit that Heaven rules. And, oh Sir, do please let me advise you. Do please start doing what you know to be right, start being kind to oppressed people—and perhaps you may be spared for longer, peaceful days.'

The king sat still for a moment, relieved in that he now knew what the dream was all about. Distressed as he had never been distressed in his life before, as he realized the grave significance of it all. Then without answering he jumped to his feet, and walked out of the room.

Nebuchadnezzar made the mistake that men have always made. He made the mistake of thinking he could slog it out with God. The mistake of thinking that he could in fact end the bout. The mistake of thinking he could step out of the ring and arrogantly answer:

'My head is bloody, but unbowed.'

Nebuchadnezzar, you imagine you saw God signal

His knock-out punch. You think you are clever enough, tough enough, to see it coming. You plan just to call it off. Nebuchadnezzar, it is God who terminates the engagement, just as it is He who commenced it.

Whenever you read your Bible, it will always help you to remember that it is God's record of His encounter with people like yourself. They enjoyed their food just as you enjoy yours (and they digested it with exactly the same enzyme mechanisms that you use to digest yours). Their hormones pushed them around just as yours push you. They liked and disliked, loved and hated, with the same intensity or lack of intensity that you and I show in our relations with our fellows. In other words, the people of the Bible are the people of today, with a difference, only, in social environment. So that when Nebuchadnezzar walked out of the encounter of the dream, he was doing just what so very many, many men have done since. Nebuchadnezzar now knew that God was after him—the great 'Hound of Heaven', to use Francis Thomson's daring analogy, was hot on his heels—but he now also knew that God's knock-out was never to beat a man into a shapeless, unresisting, helpless pulp. Rather, Nebuchadnezzar now began to realize the great blows of God are designed to stand a man up, to awake him from the dream-world of his tiny humanity and make him take his place as an 'image of God', as a creature made in the likeness of God.

And this is the very thing that man will never do, unless made to do it by the intervention of God. This is the immense greatness which is built into the one hundred and eighty (or so) pounds of chemicals that comprise a man. This is the greatness which so hardly fits man that his dust-begotten littleness will for ever seek to escape it—a greatness which constitutes the spiritual challenge of his whole life. And Nebuchadnezzar now saw that the real challenge of God is a challenge to this human feebleness, a challenge not to succumb in a retreat into nothingness, but rather to stand face to face with God, to assume finally and fully the enormous responsibility of equality with God. And though dust-begotten and creaturely, yet still to look into the face of God, to hear the voice of God, to know the will of God, and say: 'I will' *or* 'I won't'.

Nebuchadnezzar ducked, as men have always sought to duck. The great dream-punch of the loving hand of God seemed only to graze him. As he escaped into the world of his own making, he escaped into the building, the planning, the rich splendour of the Babylon he had made.

Nebuchadnezzar, you are a lucky man. You can escape into such a rich-looking, exciting-looking, worth-while-looking world. Most men can escape only into a world of golf, football, music, art, reading, fishing, horses, dogs, cinema, T.V. and the like; much of it tawdry, puny, tinsel. Yet seen for what it really is, even the snobbish distinctions we draw at our human level begin to look cheap and ridiculous. If a man is escaping God, escaping Reality, is there any real difference between escape into Beethoven and escape into rock-'n'-roll? Can you now see any real distinction between gin-rummy and contract bridge?

Nebuchadnezzar, you won't feel annoyed and upset, will you, if I ask you whether building your mighty city is really any different, except in men's eyes, from drinking ale and playing darts at the corner pub? Why, Nebuchadnezzar, I have many colleagues, very decent and conscientious medical practitioners, who do just what you are doing. They see God at work often enough; they advise patients to consult their priest, their parson; they suggest finding some help in prayer, in faith. But they themselves are too busy, their work is so valuable and humanitarian, they say, that they cannot take time off themselves to look God squarely in the face, to ask Him His will, to own Him as Master. They too, Nebuchadnezzar, are escaping.

And Nebuchadnezzar thought he had in fact got away. He had begun to forget the terrible dream. It was over a year now since that dreadful night. He had begun to wonder whether perhaps Daniel was begin-

ning to lose his grip at last. It seemed that he had
pulled quite a boner that time! As the king stood on
one of the mighty palace roof-gardens, looking out over
the huge city he had built, he was at last beginning to
feel safe. This was the real life. This was the proper
answer. Babylon. His Babylon. The Babylon, mighty
Babylon, that he had built. And not only Babylon.
This was just the centre, the capital. He owned it all.
What many a man had dreamed and hoped for, he had
in fact succeeded in attaining:

> 'He swung the earth, a trinket at his wrist.'

Nebuchadnezzar, you feel safe now, don't you? You
imagine that it is all over between you and God. That
God will just forget about you. Nebuchadnezzar, God
is not like that. God is love, and 'Love is patient, love
is kind'. But patience is not forgetfulness, kindness is
not weakness.

Nebuchadnezzar, you are not out of the ring at all.
You are still there, and there you will stay until God
Himself counts you out. Long centuries before your
time Jacob found that out, too. He had battled with
God, weaving and ducking, running now this way, now
that way. But God caught him, in a last desperate night
of struggle.

Nebuchadnezzar, Job found that out, too. He and
God had 'come to trial together', as he so graphically
puts it. But on God's terms, Nebuchadnezzar, not on
equal terms. Can't you still see the hunted look on his
face as he stares around the ring for his whole life and
exclaims in the dismay of human weakness, 'There is no
umpire between us'. No, Nebuchadnezzar, there is no
umpire, no referee; no *other* referee. This is not Madi-
son Square Gardens. This is not the crooked Big Fight
Promotion racket. Far, far from it. This is the unspeakable wonder of God and His encounter with a man He
loves. Nebuchadnezzar, God is moving up. Here He
comes!

And God knocked him down. God 'took away his
mind'. Nebuchadnezzar became a lunatic.

Yes, even as he stood there, basking in the glow of the delight of his great city—'A royal residence for the glory of my majesty' as his own lips expressed it—he heard again the voice of the dream of a year ago. While his own words were still on his lips, the voice of heaven rang in his ears: 'King Nebuchadnezzar, to you it is spoken. The kingdom has departed from you.'

And Nebuchadnezzar, the greatest king the world has ever seen, is out there in the fields, living like a beast—dishevelled, unkempt, utterly isolated by his insanity from all his fellow men. Nebuchadnezzar, king of all Babylon, is suddenly stripped of all glory, all greatness. Nebuchadnezzar is out there alone with God.

'How?' you ask. 'What happened? Was it an attack of depression? Was he paranoiac? Manic, perhaps. And they had to do this to protect him, as well as to protect the state?'

I don't know. I haven't been given enough clinical data to make a diagnosis, even if I were a psychiatrist, which I'm not. But I know this. I know that while his courtiers, his psychiatrists and his professors, and even Daniel too, were unable to communicate with him; while he was reduced to the utter loneliness of lunacy, God could still speak with him. The human mind which to fellow men is isolated in the terrible isolation of insanity, is still wide open to the loving voice of God.

And it was there, out in the fields. It was then, in the desolate pathos of the king gone clean out of his mind. It was thus, by what to our human emotional judgment seems almost the most cruel hurt that can ever be inflicted on man—it was there and then and thus that he finally met God—that the answer was given.

'My goodness!' I hear someone say. 'Just fancy that! I wonder just how it came about. I wonder if the king had some more dreams. I wonder if he heard a lot more voices and saw more exotic images, etc. This is a most interesting piece of abnormal psychological adjustment. This will prove a most valuable case for analysis for my forthcoming thesis on "Personality Breakdown—an Analysis of Historical Examples". Do go on and tell me all the details. I am dying to know just what happened.'

I am sorry. The Bible is not written as a textbook of Abnormal Psychology. It is the textbook of man *vis-à-vis* God, and all that other detail is known only to Nebuchadnezzar and to God. What did God say to Nebuchadnezzar? God hasn't told us in His Word. What did Nebuchadnezzar say to God? Nebuchadnezzar *has* told us, but he has told us only the final answer. Over the long story of the seven seasons of blackness, of insanity, a complete veil is drawn. But at the end of it all Nebuchadnezzar gave the answer that had been so long awaited by patient, relentless Love. Listen to the king now, as he is being led back on to his throne, back to the grandeur and glory of his former state. There he is, back on the roof of the same palace, where last we heard him exclaiming: 'Is not this great Babylon, which I have built by my mighty power as a royal residence and for the glory of my majesty?' Yes. He's speaking again. The same man. The same spot. The same greatness. Is it the same word he is saying? Listen. 'I, Nebuchadnezzar, lifted my eyes to heaven, and my reason returned to me, and I blessed the Most High, and praised and honoured Him who lives for ever.'

I said before that this story stirs and thrills my very heart. As I see God deliberately plan to snap the mind of a man like Nebuchadnezzar; as I see so often in my daily work, where God is taking men and women into trials and conflicts that to my human mind seem unbearable, my tiny world reels. Oh God, are You really like that? Aren't You, like us, limited and directed by emotions? Have You no feeling for our feeling? Must the game be played that way?

And I hear the strong voice of God answer quietly, firmly, 'Yes. It's not the will of the creature. It is the will of the Maker Himself. Remember, My thoughts are not your thoughts. My ways are not your ways.'

Oh God! But fancy sending a man mad! Isn't that

too awful? Isn't that going too far? Was that fair to Nebuchadnezzar?

The answer flashes back, 'Why not ask him yourself? If it wasn't fair, it is for him to say so. Ask him.'

I turn back to Nebuchadnezzar with a new interest. And as I do so, I think I see something that I have not seen in all the years we have been with him, but something I have been longing to see. Can it be true? I'll find out.

Nebuchadnezzar, will you please tell us frankly? How do you feel about the way God has treated you? Those seven seasons of insanity—what do you think of God's ways now?

And Nebuchadnezzar smiles. Yes, for the first time in all these years there is the happy smile of the man whose war with God is over, the serenity of heart of one at peace with God. 'The most wonderful thing that ever happened! God knows just how proud and stubborn I was. He knew just what was needed. I, Nebuchadnezzar!' And here all the Big King in him shows itself, as indeed it should. 'Yes, I praise and extol and honour the King of heaven. All His works are right!' Nebuchadnezzar's speech is always rather in the manner of an announcement; but this is an announcement without the bite, the bombast that we have become so used to that we notice it now only because it is missing. 'I praise and honour Him who lives for ever.'

He turns on his heel, and as he walks quickly away to attend to the vast empire that he now recognizes as the dominion of God, there is a sudden intensity of a new-found sincerity as he pauses and calls back, 'And those who walk in pride He is able to abase.'

CHAPTER FOUR

TREATMENT REFUSED

THE Ancient Greeks got rid of God very neatly by putting Him on Mount Olympus and living themselves in a happy detachment here on Evil Material Earth. Modern Man, better informed, achieves the same desirable end by putting God under Gothic arches and ecclesiastical robes, so that he may then pursue his unencumbered way in Scientific Socialized Western Society.

The Christian utterly disagrees with both, having seen how deeply God is concerned with men and their affairs. This concern is so real that He became a man —'The Word became flesh', as St. John says—in order to assume completely the responsibility and authority which belong to Him as Maker. It cost God His life to do this. It is so extremely important that He tells us He has kept in His own exclusive ownership 'every single thing that exists, visible and invisible'. Man and man's affairs come very much into this ownership, and God is mixing in with them all along the way in order to carry out His eternal plan. And so far as we are concerned, this plan may fairly be described as being a requirement by God that we make up our minds whether or not we will give to Him the particular form of wilful obedience that in the Bible is given the technical name 'faith'.

But how far will God go? Some people are 'spiritually minded'; they are constructed both genetically and environmentally with a ready capacity to appreciate the relationship of creature to Creator, and can decide in all the ordinary ways of life as to choosing to obey or to rebel. Others seem to have little such capacity. Are the former group then more favourably placed? Does God have pets? Are these the ones to whom He can readily reveal Himself? Are the others just unlucky, never having a chance to make a fair choice?

I am going to take you back to one of the textbook
cases, one of the lives God has written up in full
clinical detail; a life-story that shows us just how carefully and fairly He does work on men. In studying
this case-history we shall also find answers to a lot of
other questions which are often baffling. The tale itself
is enthralling. It is a story of adventure and danger
and war and surprise. It is not at all the simple story
about a You or a Me, not the median or the mode or
the mean, but an extreme case, taken from the far end
of the distribution curve, the case of a man who would
seem to be impossible to approach with spiritual and
religious claims. It will take us back just three thousand
years, and there in the dawn of the Iron Age teach us
how God went about His work.

How far will God go? Let us ask Saul.

The story of Saul is really like most other stories—
it begins with someone else. In his case it begins with
Samuel.

Samuel was the judge. He had been judge for years
and years, until everyone in all Israel knew about him,
and knew that Jehovah had revealed Himself to
Samuel. Every year the old man went on circuit. To
Bethel; then to Gilgal; then to Mizpah, giving judg-
ments concerning the problems of the people in those
cities. And then home to Ramah, where he lived and
had his centre of administration and judgment. He
had become better known than anyone since Moses and
Joshua.

In fact everyone knew Samuel. Everyone, that is,
except Saul. Saul didn't need to know Samuel. He was
doing very nicely, thank you, in his father's prosperous
donkey business. They were not in a big way, just a
nice compact little stud, but they were quite well off
and had no need to call up prophets and judges and
the like.

Now do not think less of Saul for that. He was
young, very good-looking, highly intelligent, rich, and
happy on his father's farm. They were honest, straight-

forward people who had no crooked deals on their
hands, and no law-suits to tangle them up with Samuel
the judge. Saul just didn't need anything more. He was
happy enough if God kept Samuel in His corner of
the ring, while Saul and his dad kept donkeys in theirs.
God and Samuel. Saul and asses.

Now Saul was no fool at all. He was no more foolish
than the majority of men today, who think God is
deeply interested in Church and Sunday-school, and
perhaps the Red Cross or Rotary; but not in banking,
rheumatism, examinations, street accidents or family
affairs. In fact not many Christians even are clear in
their minds as to how precisely God is involved in
the tiny details of every single happening in life.
They are not fools, any more than Saul was a fool.
Like him, they just don't know how ready God is
to mix Himself with them in their lives. He is the
Maker, and it is the right and the requirement of
the Creator to show the creature just what He wants.
I don't need to go looking for God. It is up to Him
to find me. Saul was not—repeat *not*—looking for
God.

So God did the obvious thing with Saul. He got into
the donkey-business Himself. He lost Saul's donkeys
for him!

Saul was now involved properly. Of course he hadn't
a clue that he was mixed up with God. He thought it
was only a case of a stupid farm-hand leaving the rail
out of the fence gate and the donkeys are out and now
we'll have to go and find the silly animals what a
thorough pest I'd like to kick that idiot come on then
let's get going. . . .

So Saul is off to chase up the lost donkeys, taking a
good herdsman with him. These donkeys are valuable;
and Saul is no quitter. In three days he has searched all
the hills of Ephraim, gone through Shalisha and
Shaalim, trekked across all Benjamin and is now out
of food and cash near Zuph.

'Well, that's that,' said Saul to the herdsman; 'we'll
have to give up. After all this time Dad will stop

worrying about the donkeys and start worrying about us. Let's give up and go home.'

The herdsman was not a religious genius, but he was a short step ahead of his master. 'But look,' he replied, 'there is a man of God in this city. He has a great reputation. He can tell you things. Couldn't we go up and ask him for his help and advice?'

Saul was sceptical, and a bit uneasy. He was sound enough in the live-stock business, but not in religion. He was in trouble, but he would rather get himself out of it. Calling in the help of prophets may get a man involved in religion or something.

'Hm . . . I don't know.' Then he saw it couldn't work. 'But how can we make a deal? We haven't any money and not even any bread left in our knapsacks to pay him with. It looks as if we're stuck there.'

Not the servant. 'I've got a quarter of a silver shekel (about two shillings). I don't mind giving him that.'

'Oh,' said Saul, 'have you? I suppose that might do. It doesn't seem much, but it will probably be enough for a prophet. Come on, then. Let's go.' A couple of bob was a fair enough price then as now for spiritual advice. Pass round the collection plate and we will do the fair and decent thing.

As they turned to go up to Zuph, they met some young women coming down to the well.

'Is the seer here?' they asked.

'He is,' said the women. 'Go straight up, and you'll meet him right away.'

How simple it all sounds. How simple it really is, for God.

The day before, God had told Samuel that Saul was coming, and the old prophet was sitting in the gateway to the town, so that he would be the first person Saul met as he came in.

'Excuse me, Sir, but could you tell me if the seer lives here?'

'Yes,' said Samuel. 'I am the seer. I am waiting for you. And let me put you at ease concerning the donkeys. They are found, so stop worrying. You can stay the night with me and go home in the morning. But I have first some very great favours from God to convey to you.'

Saul was nonplussed, as well he might be. His alert brain was racing: I should have known better than to come here. I don't want favours from God. I only want the asses. How can I politely back out of this now?

'Oh, I think there must be some mistake,' he stammered. 'I appreciate very much the news of the donkeys. That is very kind of you. But I don't need favours from God. I'm a member of a very humble family and from the smallest tribe in all Israel. You must have me mixed up with someone else, surely.'

But Samuel had been too long in the game to be put off as simply as that. Firmly he took Saul and his servant, and led them to his home.

More astonishment, and more embarrassment. About thirty guests were seated at a banquet, with the place of honour at the head of the table left vacant for Saul to take!

'Cook,' called Samuel. 'Bring in the special serving I told you to set aside.'

In came the cook with the finest selected cuts of meat.

'Look,' said Samuel to Saul. 'Here is the special cut I had put aside for you. Now do enjoy a good meal, because it is a banquet particularly arranged for you to meet some of these V.I.P.s.'

Hm . . . These donkeys! Ten minutes ago Saul couldn't have picked out Samuel from any other old man in the city any more than you or I could pick out one long-eared donkey from another. And now here he is at the head of the old man's table, being fêted by a select group of thirty guests. It's almost as if a complete stranger to church is suddenly found as Chairman of the Promotion Scheme; the People's Warden; or perhaps on the Fellowship Committee. That's the trouble with God. He knows all the answers, and is always one jump ahead of us.

That night Saul was given a bed specially made up

on the roof of Samuel's house, a place of great honour
in the hot summer.

I wonder how well Saul slept. . . .

The next morning Samuel woke him early, and
walked down the road with him. As they came to the
outskirts of the town, the prophet said: 'Tell your
servant to go ahead a bit. When he is out of sight I
will tell you what God has said.'

When they were alone, Samuel stopped. Deliberately,
very seriously, with that disconcerting directness Saul
was to come to know so well, the old man took out a
vial of oil, poured it over the young farmer's head, and
kissed him. 'God has anointed you to be prince over
His people Israel. You are to reign over them, and
God will save you from the hand of your enemies.'

Saul's ears are tingling, his head is spinning. Twenty-
four hours ago he was a simple farmer looking for lost
donkeys. Now he is anointed first king of Israel. He is
bewildered, incredulous. Samuel watches him closely,
his shrewd mind reading the young man's thoughts and
fears as if written in capital letters. He admires Saul's
fine appearance, sympathizes with him in his anxiety,
but never wavers in his clear and incisive instructions.

'And this will be the proof to you that all this is true.
Firstly—when you leave me you will meet two men
near Rachel's Tomb at Zelzah. They will say to you,
"The asses you went looking for are found, and your
father has lost interest in them, and is worried about
you." Secondly—you will come to an oak tree at
Tabor. There three men will meet you, on their way
up to Bethel. You can't possibly miss them, because
one of them will be carrying three loaves of bread,
another will be carrying three kids, and the third a skin
of wine. They will stop and talk to you, and give you
two loaves of bread. You are to take them. Thirdly—
you will come to Gibeathelohim, where the Philistine
garrison is. There you will meet a band of prophets
coming down from worship, playing their musical
instruments and prophesying. Now listen carefully.
The Spirit of God will come upon you dramatically,

and you will prophesy with them. In fact you will become a new sort of man altogether.

'Now then. Those three signs are clear enough, and should show you that God is with you. Goodbye now, and I will meet you again later. . . .'

Those donkeys, did you say?

Saul set off, speechless. And it all happened. The message about the asses. The three men and their assorted loads and the two loaves for Saul. The bands of prophets. And particularly the prophets, because Saul himself turned into a prophet! The man who the day before had never met a prophet, and couldn't care less, was now one of them. His friends, for he was now near home, were astonished. 'What's happened to Kish's son?' everyone asked. 'Fancy him getting religious. Fancy a prophet in the Kish family. Wonders will never cease!'

Saul was bothered. This was really going too far. And he wasn't to be the last one bothered like that, either. 'Look at Jonesey. Going to church! What do y'know?' 'Hey, Gus. You know what? Wait till I tell yer. Joe's gorn religious. Says he went to a mission and got converted. Ha ha. Come and see Blue's face when I tell him.' 'John, dear. I'm worried about Tony. He told me today he has joined the Evangelical Union or some awful name like that at the University and I'm sure you should have a serious talk to him about it. In our position. . . .' Saul was certainly not the last.

But Saul was still not entirely convinced. He was shaken. He was changed. But he still had his own ideas on what to do with his own life. Those donkeys had led him no end of a dance, and God had caught up with him a bit, but he still knew how to look after himself. He met one of his uncles as he was near home (call him Uncle Joe—his name is not recorded).

'Hello, Saul.'

'Hello, Uncle Joe.'

'Where have you been? I didn't expect to see you round these parts, I thought you would be busy looking after those fine donkeys of your Dad.'

'Well, that's where I have been. The donkeys got lost.'

'Goodness me. Did they? Couldn't you find them?'

'Oh, it's all right. The donkeys are found. I'm on my way home now. I've hunted them all over the place.'

'I'm glad to hear that. Are you sure they are found? You haven't got them with you.'

'No, they are safe. As a matter of fact we met Samuel, and he told us they were found.'

'Ho!' said Uncle Joe. 'Samuel, eh? Do tell me what *he* said. I've never actually spoken to the old boy, but I'd love to know what Samuel said.'

'He is really quite good,' said Saul. 'He is surprisingly clear in what he says.' (Most people think God always talks terribly vaguely, in Elizabethan English with a deep parsonical voice.) 'He told me quite plainly that the asses were found, and I could come home.'

But about the matter of the kingdom, about which Samuel had also spoken clearly, he did not tell his uncle anything.

'Thanks for the donkeys; but none of this kingdom business. I can see how useful God can be if He likes. But I must keep to that. There is a limit.'

Saul returned to his farm.

Now there is a lot of local history wrapped up with the story of Saul. There is a lot of local history wrapped up in the story of anyone. I am only middle-aged (I think), but there are two world wars, one depression, years of cold war, and men in space already wrapped in mine. In fact history is really just the accumulated stories of how God is working in the lives of all the individual people on earth.

In Saul's time, the tribes-people of Israel were wanting a king. They had been nearly five hundred years in Palestine now, and were still precariously perched on the tops of the mountain ranges, too poor to live more than hand to mouth, too weak to capture the fertile plains down below them. Lots of them got sick of this, and sold themselves into servitude to the surrounding nations, preferring this bondage to the endless uncertainty of such a life as they had in freedom. Finally the people got together and came and told Samuel they wanted a king. It was really a vote of no-confidence, cast primarily against God, but more directly against Samuel and his sons. But God had spoken to Samuel, and told him to agree to it.

And now Samuel has met Saul, and has anointed him to be this first king. No-one else knows a thing about it. Not the herdsman, not Uncle Joe, not the family, certainly not the nation. Only Samuel and Saul. And of these two, Samuel didn't approve of kings in general, and Saul didn't approve of himself being king in particular! It was a well-kept secret.

Then came the day for the selection of the king. All the leaders of all the tribes met, and started on the process of ballot. They did not use the system of secret ballot, which is so open to abuse and crooked electioneering, but the simpler and fairer system of lots. First, tribes—the lot fell on Benjamin. Now families—the family of the Matrites. Heads of families—Kish. Which son in the family?—Saul. Saul is king! Hurrah for Saul! Who is Saul? I don't know. Never heard of him. But he's king, and that's the main thing. Three cheers for Saul!

But where is Saul? Everyone is here except Saul. Hey, Samuel, where is this fellow? Are you sure you've picked the right man? What's all this? We can't find any Saul!

So Samuel asks God again—and gets the astonishing reply, 'He has hidden himself among the baggage.' The new king hiding? Surely not! But he is. He's hiding all right. Then why, is he scared? Is he incompetent? Is he a little runt of a fellow who could never be a leader? No. Saul is really a great man, brave, shrewd, strong, everything a king should be. Then is he just too modest? Not at all. He is modest, but it is the modesty of a great man aware of his greatness.

No, of course. That is not why Saul is hiding. He is hiding because of what the donkeys taught him. They

had taught him how easily God can interfere in life.
And he still preferred to keep going along without
God.

And now he is cornered. The people rush to the
baggage, and bring out the new king. And what a
king! Head and shoulders taller than any of them. The
best looker, the best built, the best choice. 'And all the
people shouted, "Long live the king!"'

Saul is king. One day a donkey-breeding farmer. The
next a prophet. Next week, the king.

Does God know what He is doing? Let us see.

Samuel sent the people back to their homes, and
Saul, King Saul, went back to his farm.

Now what?

Now back to local history. Up in the north, Nahash,
an Ammonite, besieged the little town of Jabesh. The
townspeople could see no way of release or escape, so
finally they said to Nahash, 'All right, you win. Make
a treaty with us, and we will serve you.' 'How right
you are,' replied Nahash. 'I will make a treaty with
you. I certainly will. And on these terms. Are you
listening carefully? I'll make a treaty with you that will
make you and all the rest of you Israelites look silly.
My terms are that you will let me gouge out all your
right eyes!'

Whew! I must say that as a doctor I vote a strong
no! So did the people of Jabesh! The aldermen of
the town said, 'Give us a week to think that one over.
And if no-one rescues us, then we are for it.' It is one
of the most cruel and sadistic stories in all history, and
when news of it came to the people of Israel they all
cried with fear and shame.

Saul was out ploughing when the news reached him.
He stopped his oxen, and said to the messengers,
'What's the matter? What are you all crying about?'
So they told him of the terrible plight of the people of
Jabesh. Saul was mad with rage. No tears here, but the
strong anger of a great man who sees a great wrong. He
strode up to his yoked oxen, and cut them into pieces.
Taking the still warm flesh, he thrust the pieces into

the hands of the runners, and said, 'Go right through the country and tell every man Jack you see that if he doesn't come to Samuel and Saul he will have his oxen destroyed like this!'

The people were galvanized by such leadership. They streamed in—thirty thousand from his own tribe alone. Three hundred thousand from the others. One morning before dawn this huge army descended in three echelons upon Nahash and his Ammonites and utterly crushed them. 'No two of them were left together.'

Saul is king. And now he knows what it feels like. He knows the sort of help he can rely on. Perhaps it's not as bad as he had feared. Perhaps he can be king and still go his own way after all. 'Perhaps that's all there is in it,' he says to himself. 'I'll try and make a go of it, and be a real king. But I rather wish old Samuel would soft-pedal his stuff a bit, and just leave it to me to run the show the way I like it. Listen to him out there now, haranguing this army I collected. . . .'

'. . . And I will never cease to pray for you, and I will instruct you in the good and right way. Only fear the Lord, and serve Him faithfully with all your heart. Just consider what great things He has done for you. But if you still do wickedly, you shall be swept away, both you and your king.'

That's just the trouble, isn't it, Saul? You are king, but you are still tangled with Samuel. Never mind. It won't be for long. Samuel is old, and won't last much longer. Then you will be free to go ahead on your own. Is that what you think? How silly can you get? God will get Samuel out of your life so that He may come in Himself!

Let us go on with the story, and see how God did it.

Saul raised a standing army of three thousand men. Two thousand he stationed with himself at Michmash, and the other thousand he put under his son Jonathan at Gibeah. And it was young Jonathan who blew the main fuse. He took his battalion and destroyed the

Philistine garrison at Geba! The fat is really in the
fire!

I hope you are not thinking of the Philistines as
being like the Ammonites under Nahash. The Ammonites are just a local tribe, strong and tough enough in
their own little piece of country. But the Philistines
are one of the great world powers, one of the Big
Names in history. They were the iron makers of the
world, they were fighters to a man. You should talk
about Philistines in the way you talk about the Egyptians, the Greeks, the Romans, the British. And Jonathan, the daring young spark, had been reckless enough
to clean up one of their outpost garrisons. It is almost
as though a band of American Indians had blown up
West Point.

The Philistine H.Q. heard soon enough, and didn't
like what they heard. They called for a general mobili-
zation. Up they rolled with thirty thousand chariots, six
thousand horsemen, and so many infantry that they
couldn't count them! Up they streamed and camped
opposite Saul at Michmash.

Saul was not distressed. He was brave and clever, and
he had only recently had three hundred and thirty
thousand men coming at his call.

'Let the Hebrews hear,' said Saul. 'Rally! Rally!'
He retreated to Gilgal and waited for the crowd to
come pouring in. Samuel sent word: 'Wait at Gilgal,
and on the seventh day I will come and join you, and
offer the sacrifices. And I will tell you what to do.'
Jonathan came, with his thousand men. Saul had his
two thousand, of course. That made three thousand.

So Saul waited. And waited. And waited. No-one
came. No-one. Only the three thousand he started with.
Three thousand? Doesn't look like that today. The
next day there seem less still. Getting fewer and fewer.
By the seventh day it's down to well under a thousand.
Even the standing army are in a blue funk. They're
deserting. They are hiding in caves, in holes in the
ground, in graves, in wells, they are even sneaking
across the Jordan to escape. And the few still with Saul

'followed him trembling'. Saul is worried. He is in a real jam. No troops. And worse still, no weapons! He himself has a sword and a spear. And Jonathan has the same. But that's all. Two swords and two spears and a few hundred trembling troops, staring across the valley at thirty thousand chariots plus. And not even Samuel to give the men a pep talk.

Ah! but that is it! Of course! He will do that himself. Religion can be wonderful tactics. He'll call a Church Parade. And he will offer the burnt offering and the peace offering himself. . . . And just as he was finishing, who should walk up but Samuel, looking very old and very stern.

Samuel walked straight up to him and greeted him with a terse 'What have you done?'

Saul was getting used to Samuel and his directness, and has his answer pat. 'Why, I could see that the men were terrified and scattering, and there are the Philistines stacked up at Michmash, and you weren't here, and of course I knew I should entreat the favour of Jehovah, so I felt I just had to go ahead and offer the sacrifices myself.'

It seemed reasonable. It was a desperate situation, and God (and Samuel) would surely see that it was reasonable.

The old prophet looked him square in the face, and spoke bitterly and bluntly. 'You have behaved like a fool. You had your instructions very clearly from God, and you have not obeyed them. This way you lose the kingdom. If you will not obey God, then He has someone else who will, and God will give that man your kingdom. Now you think that over. So far as I am concerned, you are through. You are on your own. Goodbye.'

Saul has got free of Samuel at last. But Saul is now scared. He counts his men, carefully this time. Only six hundred. He re-checks his armaments. Still only two swords and two spears. No need to try and count the Philistines. They can't even count them themselves! What a mess!

Jonathan is the only man in the whole set-up who is not a bit bothered. It is largely on his account that all this trouble has arisen, but he is quite unperturbed. He says to his armour-bearer, but not so loudly that Saul can hear him, 'Come on. Let us go over to the Philistine garrison on the other side of the valley.' What a man! These Philistine garrisons seemed to draw him like a magnet! So off these two went, without anyone in the camp noticing it. Off they headed for the enemy camp.

Keeping carefully under cover, they came near to the enemy lines. Jonathan stopped. 'What say we go on?' he asked his companion. 'I am sure God can fight with a few just as easily as with many. Are you game?'

'You're the one to say,' said the soldier. 'I'll do anything you ask.'

'Right. Now what say we let them see us? Then if they say, "Hey, you fellows. Wait there. We will come across and talk to you", then we go for our lives, because we will know God doesn't want us to fight them. But if they say, "Hey! come over here and talk to us", we will go, and take it that God has delivered them into our hands.'

Isn't Jonathan delightful? I must say that the best bit of Saul's story is Jonathan's bit.

So the two bobbed up from behind the rocks, and the Philistines saw them.

'Just look!' yelled the Philistines. 'The Hebrews are popping up out of the holes they have been hiding in. Hi-ya, rats! Don't you like it in your funk holes? Come over here, and we will show you a thing or two.'

'Come on,' said Jonathan. 'God has given them into the hands of Israel.' And the two men clambered up hand over fist to attack the whole Philistine army.

I sometimes wish the Old Testament writers had had a course in modern journalism. So often they merely jot down the barest headlines and omit entirely all the spicy tit-bits and editorials and the like. There has never been a better tale of Commando tactics than in this story, and it is all down in one line: 'They fell before Jonathan, and his armour-bearer killed them after him.' That's all. It's only a garrison of Philistines, only about a quarter of a million more where they came from. So simple, these two doing a bit of landing assault tactics stuff on their own. They are coming up a defile in the rocks, a narrow pass with a sheer rock-face on either side. It only lasts a minute or two. It couldn't last much longer, of course. Two against a quarter of a million, plus chariots, plus horsemen, is the sort of thing that is good while it lasts, but it doesn't last.

But wait a minute. What has happened? Jonathan is still there. In this narrow defile, he is getting them. A quick leap, his foot under a Philistine ankle, a low tackle, and the man crashes on his face. Plunk! goes the spear of the armour-bearer into the falling Philistine, and that's one of them at least. Another leap, a twist, a quick duck as the Philistine lunges with his big heavy iron sword, a shove and he's down. Plunk! That's another. And another. . . . Plunk! Nineteen. Plunk! Twenty. . . . And that's all. What did you say? Twenty? I thought you said there were about a quarter of a million and rows of chariots and what-not. Twenty is nothing. It's only been going about two minutes, only about a hundred feet of advance. Yes, but that is all.

Jonathan spins round another ledge. No-one there! Just a glimpse of a Philistine back, the back view of a man scrambling away in sheer terror. No-one else in sight. But there is a thundering row going on up the hill. Men shouting. Boots kicking and slithering on the loose stones. More shouting. Swords clanging on the rocks. Shouting and yelling. Chariot wheels rumbling. Screams with the shouts, as of men being run over. Horses' hooves beating in full gallop. Cries, groans, and always the swelling roar of human voices shouting in the terrible grip of panic.

Yes. That is all it took. Two men doing a bit of the sort of fighting they were good at—mountain fighting, where a stick or a club is safe, where heavy iron armour and big iron swords mean death to the owner. And the

Philistines panicked. The panic spread like a bush-fire.
The thirty thousand chariots became just so many
weapons of death as terrified men leap aboard to
escape; or fail to leap aboard and are run into the
ground.

It's a tremendous story. I wish I could stop and
work out more of it with you, but not now. There is
a lot more in it about Jonathan and how he followed
the enemy all that day; there is the story of the people
who came out of their hiding places and joined in the
hunt; there is particularly the story of Saul, who saw
trouble among the Philistines and leaped after them
with his now unrestrainable men; there is the story of
trouble between Saul and Jonathan that day, a miserable story if ever there was one. It's a tremendous story
all right. It was a wonderful day. I don't think there
has ever been any day like that in all the history of
war—a day when two men routed the whole army of
one of the world's great powers.

And now Saul can see it all. Even Saul, the self-
possessed Saul, sure of himself and aloof from God, is
bowed in awe. That night Saul did what he had never
done before. He did what every man must do some
day. 'Saul built an altar to the Lord. It was the first
altar that he built to the Lord.'

Yes. God has got through to Saul at last. The donkey
farmer who lived quietly in his little tribe and kept
safely out of God's way, has been beaten. He has lost
the donkeys, he has lost Samuel, he is now on his own
in the presence of God alone. God has got him where
He wants him. It was tough going. God had to do an
awful lot of history-making to reach him. But now all
that is over.

'Saul,' said God. 'You are now talking to Me. This
is not just you and your father and asses. Not you and
the prophets and four actual experiences of prophesying. Not you and Samuel and Philistines. This is now
you and Me. Saul, am I right?'

'Yes. Only too right, Lord. That's why I built this
altar.'

'Good. Now, Saul. I made you king over Israel. That was My doing. And I am giving you, as king, My instructions. I want you to go and destroy the Amalekites. I do not want you to spare anything whatever. Every man, woman, child, and baby in arms. Every ox, sheep, camel and ass. Everything they have. I want them utterly destroyed. Is that clear? Do you understand the instructions?'

'Yes. That is clear enough.'

'Then away you go.'

This is it, then. Saul has met God. He has built his altar, he has been in the divine Presence. And now God is asking for obedience. Saul thinks it over. And the more he thinks it over the less he likes it. I think it is the bit about the asses. 'God, that is crazy. I know a lot about asses. And other farm animals too, of course. These are prize stock, and just to kill them is plain silly. Why, even if we keep them for sacrifices, they will still not be wasted. That's what I'll do. I'll bring back the really good stock, and use them up on sacrifices. And I'll bring back Agag, their king, so that he can watch his animals sacrificed to Jehovah. Now isn't that a good idea? That should please You very much, God. Wouldn't You like Agag to see how very highly we rate You in Israel? Show him his best stock going up in smoke because we trust so much in You? I'll watch his face and see him squirm. Yes, that is a very much better plan. That is what I'll do.'

And that is what he did.

And God said, 'Has the Lord as great delight in burnt offerings and sacrifices, as in obeying the voice of the Lord? Look! To obey is better than sacrifice. . . . Because you have rejected the word of the Lord, he has also rejected you.'

That is the end. Saul's story is over. Saul is still there, going on as king for many years, ending his life at his own hand on the battle-field fighting the Philistines. But with God the story is over long before that. It was Saul who ended it, and in the way that any man may end his encounter with God. 'My mind and will are determined. I will run my own life, thank you. I can do better for myself than God can do for me.'

How far will God go? That is how far He will go. Never less than that. No need to go further. You and I are being involved with God and by God in just the same way. And so are the Smiths and the Joneses and the Browns, the whites and the blacks and the yellows and the others who make up humanity. God is revealing Himself to us all, and only ever to ask the same burning question: 'Will you give Me that willing obedience that you now know is My due?'

God has done that to me. I met Him first, as far as I can remember, when I was a small boy. 'Lad,' He said; 'I am willing to take over the whole responsibility of your life. Will you be willing just to follow Me?' I met Him last as I sat here re-reading this paragraph as I typed it. 'John Hercus,' He is saying. 'Will you still say that? All the life beyond hangs on your choice. Are you still following obediently? Don't forget Saul. The more he knew Me and knew about Me the more he dug his toes in against Me. The more he saw the One whom he was up against, the more he fought back. Remember Pharaoh? He did the same. Every move I made in his life simply confirmed his opposition to Me. It only hardened his heart further. Well, then? Are you still following Me? Now that you know so much more of what I am planning, is that boyhood decision of yours still valid?'

'Yes, Lord. The decision still holds, and a thousand times more now than then. Saul has terrified me. His story has made me more willing than ever to obey You, to let You take over my life. Please be so gracious and clear in teaching that I may learn to "count everything as loss because of the surpassing worth of knowing Christ Jesus my Lord".'

CHAPTER FIVE

THE TREATMENT WORKS

Now the story of any man really begins with mum and dad. And of course their stories begin with each grandma and grandad; or perhaps better still, with the great-grandmas and great-grandads. In fact, it properly goes back to the beginning of all stories, to God Himself.

Our particular story concerns the life of Joseph. It must at least go back to great-grandad, for he was quite a man, and he had himself been through an enormous psychological mill. He was a citizen of one of the greatest and most stable civilizations in all history, when God rooted him out, and made him become a nomad, a bedouin. He was Abram, living in Ur of the Chaldees; and he became Abraham, the homeless wanderer.

Now what this did to Abram's psyche is nobody's business. He developed into a strong, dominant, towering figure; but one who must have been very hard to live with. And to add to his complexes was the tragedy of having no son. In his intensely patriarchal culture, where to have sons is to be rich and to have no son is to be pitiably poor, he is childless. He is getting old, and his wife is no chicken either—and no heir. And he is too late now. He can't possibly become a father in his old age, and his wife Sarah has long since passed her menopause—and no son.

But God had promised him a son. That was part of the story of going out of Ur, and becoming a nomad. God made that part of the issue: 'You do what I tell you, and I'll guarantee your future' was the essence of God's command, and how could a man in that society talk of the future when he had no son? Of course it meant a son.

And the son came! Wonder of wonders, Isaac was born! Sarah couldn't believe it, when she realized she was pregnant. In fact she laughed outright, when she first had it suggested to her. And Abraham had grinned rather sheepishly, though I don't think he was as much surprised as he was delighted. But it was a boy, and he was called Isaac.

Now you don't need to be a successful psychologist to guess what happened to Isaac. The fussing and the turmoil in the home has rarely been equalled. You read the story of Hagar and Ishmael, and see what happened to Isaac. His boyhood was just the textbook list of complexes; he is as up-and-down as one emotional being can get. And security, in its proper sense, is just clean out of his experience.

But if his boyhood was terrible enough, in adolescence the blow really fell. A bad start became a total wreck.

He was just at the age where he might perhaps begin to find his own feet, begin to be a man, when his dad blew all the fuses. Sternly, very grimly, and in great sadness of heart, one day Abraham took the youth off with him into a lonely mountain. They had started off with a couple of servants, but these were now a long way behind. The two of them trudged on, alone. Isaac knew they were going to worship, and he knew that when they went to worship they always went to sacrifice. So he was not a bit surprised when they got to the top of the mountain to see his father begin to start making a place for sacrifice. Stones, a heap of stones. Sticks, a heap of sticks, on top of the stones. 'Ah,' thought Isaac, 'I wonder what's special about it all. I wonder why we've come out here to do all this. It looks just like a sacrifice, just like an ordinary one. I really hoped it was going to be something rather unusual. I wonder why Dad has come away out here just to sacrifice. I don't suppose he'll tell me. He doesn't ever talk much. Oh! I wonder what he's going to sacrifice! He didn't bring any sheep or goat. Hey, Dad! You haven't got a sacrifice. Where is the animal?'

And as he said it he knew. He didn't need to see the tense drawn look on his father's old face, to get his answer. He didn't need to hear the words that came almost incoherently from his father's lips, 'God will provide a sacrifice.' The averted eyes, the short, heaving breath that seemed to shake Dad's body, told Isaac everything.

And he couldn't resist, as his father picked him up and put him on top of the altar. His tongue was simply unable to move in his parched mouth, as he was bound in a place of sacrifice. His whole life seemed to ebb away, as with starting eyes he saw his father take up a cruel knife to end it all.

Poor Isaac. Poor Abraham. What a day! 'Yes,' I think you say, 'but it turned out all right in the end.' What on earth do you mean, 'it turned out all right'? What adolescent can come through such an episode and be all right? What father can go through such an episode and be the same? Why, God says Abraham was nowhere near the same. He says Abraham came out one hundred per cent, completely right, justified—after this. And Isaac came out of it with an emotional insecurity that could hardly be paralleled.

But I must get on with the story; because it is not Abraham's story, nor Isaac's story, that we are wanting to study. Isaac is the grandfather of the man we are looking at, and we really haven't seen anything, until we have seen the father. Abraham may have been a bundle of complexes; Isaac may have been a positive wobbling jelly of insecurities; but Dad is a million times worse than both of them.

For Dad is Jacob. Crooked, twisted-up Jacob. One of Isaac's sons. Isaac had been found a most beautiful girl, Rebecca, for a wife, but he had had none of the emotional satisfaction and sense of achievement of having wooed and won her. Abraham had had a servant go and bring her from his old home town in the Chaldean nation. Rebecca is given to Isaac. And she had twin sons.

The first twin born was a big, red, red-headed baby and of course they called him Esau, which was their word for red. And clinging to his heel, in what to the

obstetricians is a very difficult delivery (a hand and
shoulder presentation), is the second twin. Thank
goodness he's tiny, or he would never have been born
at all. And of course he is called Jacob, which is their
word for 'the one who takes by the heel'—what we
would call 'the tripper-up-er.'

And what a heart-breaking all-time record of a mess
this turns into!

Esau, the elder twin, is everything Dad had himself
wanted to be. Big, tough, game, a fine huntsman, and
a regular he-man. He can get out into the grasslands
and bring down a deer. Venison is his contribution to
the household economy. And what venison! Savoury,
cooked to perfection—everything a father could wish.
Isaac would sit there in his tent, getting old now, not
seeing very much lately as cataract or something be-
mists his old eyes. But Esau would be out hunting, and
would soon be back with the venison, and he could
sniff its lovely, savoury smell wafting into the open tent.
And Esau would come in with it himself and Isaac
would take it from his big strong hands, feel the lovely
male hairiness of his wrists, and delight to the deep
bass voice and rich resounding laugh of the elder son.
Yes, Esau is all Isaac wanted. His own life had turned
out weak and pitiful, he would admit to himself. (Of
course he had made a lot of cash, and owned no end of
flocks and what-not. But that was nothing—those dull-
witted Hittites and Phoenicians were no match for his
shrewd farming and business abilities, and he almost
felt a bit apologetic about all that.) But Esau made up
for it all, now. And when it came to giving the blessing,
which went to the eldest son by right, he would really
make it a blessing to end all blessings.

And Jacob is Mother's favourite, and is just about
the hopeless case. Shrewd, high I.Q., jealous of Esau
and his big toughness, Jacob is in the kitchen helping
Mum. She and Dad don't have anything much in
common now. He likes Esau, she likes Jacob. And while
cheery big Esau goes whistling and singing along his
happy hunting way, Rebecca is in the tent with Jacob,

wondering what she can do to help the little fellow. Thinking up schemes to get the second boy on top. And Jacob is scheming too. And scheming. And scheming. And scheming. . . .

And a chance turns up.

Esau came home one day, dog-tired, hungry as any hunter should be. Jacob had a dish of very good-looking and good-smelling dinner there, just ready to be devoured. 'How about some, young fellow? I could eat a horse. I'd give anything for a dish like that!' 'Sure', said Jacob, 'I'll swop you this for your birthright.'

Esau looked up, surprised. 'Birthright?' he replied. 'What birthright? Oh, you mean my birthright. I'd clean forgotten about that. I don't know that I really know what it is. But I do know I'm famished. Okay, it's a deal. You give me that dish of good-oh, and you can have the birthright.'

But the birthright is not the main thing at all. It is the blessing that goes with it that really matters. This is a society and a culture where father-son and son-father relationships are the only ones that really count. Oh, yes, Jacob has had Mum on his side, sure enough, and he still has. But it is the father's blessing that carries all the weight. If only he can get this out of Dad, beat Esau to the blessing, then he has really won the day. That would compensate for all the hateful misery he has been enduring all his life—the agony of being second, when he is just burning up in his desire to be first. The deep emotional longing to be first in Isaac's eyes, the only eyes really worth anything. To be free from the humiliation of being acceptable only to Mother.

And then the time for dreaming and musing was at an end. And action, plenty of action was called for.

One day Rebecca heard a murmur of voices coming from Isaac's tent. And being Rebecca, she tip-toed over to eavesdrop. And what she heard left her trembling in anxiety and concern. Blind old Isaac was calling out, 'Son. My son.' It was Esau who called back, 'Yes,

Dad. Here I am.' 'I am getting very old,' the pathetic
old man went on, 'and my time is nearly up. Now you
take your weapons, your bow and arrows, and go and
hunt game for me; and prepare a savoury dish, such as
I love, and bring it to me to eat; and then I will bless
you—before I die.'

Rebecca was stunned. But only for a minute. 'Jacob,'
she called to the second twin, as soon as Esau had left
for the hunt. 'Jacob, quickly. Get me two good kids
from the flock, and I'll make a savoury dish like the
one Esau makes for your father. And you take it in and
tell him you're Esau, and get the Blessing. Quickly,
don't just stand there! Run!'

'But Mother, Esau is covered with hair, and I am
not. If my father touches me, he'll find out, and then he
will curse me, not bless me.'

'Then let the curse be mine. Just do as I tell you.
But hurry, hurry!'

Jacob ran and brought in the two kids, while
Rebecca prepared the special dish. Then she took
Esau's best suit, and put it on Jacob. She took some of
the skins of the kids, and covered his hands and neck,
gave him the dish and sent him in to Isaac.

'Father,' called Jacob, from the tent door—I think
in a quavery falsetto, trying to sound basso profundo.

'Yes. Who is it? Is it my son? Which son is this?'
Isaac was tensed.

'I am Esau, your first-born. I have brought you the
dish of game. Now sit up and eat it, then bless me.'

Isaac was still unprepared. 'How did you get it so
quickly, my son?' 'Because your God made me successful.' Isaac's head was swimming a little, I think. 'Come
near, and let me feel you. I must be sure you are really
Esau.'

Jacob came up to the old man, who felt his hands,
all furry with the kid-skin covering. 'The voice is
Jacob's voice, but the hands are the hands of Esau.
But . . . are you really my son, Esau?'

'I am,' answered Jacob firmly.

'Then bring me the food to eat. After that I will

bless you.' And Jacob brought the food and the old man ate it up.

What a miserable, wretched set-up it was. It looks very sadly as though the key to the blessing lies in the venison stew. As Alexander Whyte once said, this whole tale 'reeks of venison'. For now, even this pseudo-venison, cooked and prepared by a cunning and unscrupulous wife, is able to win the old man's conviction.

'Now, come and kiss me, my son.'

Jacob need not have feared to come so close—his mother was up to all the tricks. Isaac may have been blind, but he could still feel, and he could still smell. His hands felt the hairy lamb-skin on the back of Jacob's neck, and his nose told him that the clothes were the clothes of a man of the field. And out poured the words of blessing: wishing him wealth, comfort, plenty. And 'be Lord over your brethen; and may your mother's sons bow down to you'.

It was all the blessing the old man could conjure up. Savoury venison called from him everything he could think of.

Jacob was barely out of the tent, before Esau arrived. He burst in with his steaming dish of savoury food. 'Father, would you like to sit up first, and eat the game I have caught? And after that you may bless me.'

Isaac blanched. 'Who are you?' he called thickly.

'I am Esau, your first-born.'

The old man started to tremble violently. 'Then who was it who hunted game, and brought it to me. I ate it all before you came . . . and I blessed him. . . .' The old man's voice began to quaver. 'And he shall be blessed!' he cried out in sudden vehemence as he remembered the potency and significance of the patriarchal blessing.

A great thunder of rage burst from Esau. Rage mixed with fear. 'But bless me, father. Me, too, father.'

What a scene. What a family. What a story of sadness, and treachery, and misery. Esau, we read, the strong, tough Esau, 'lifted up his voice and wept. Esau hated Jacob'.

Rebecca knew what Esau felt and thought. She had known all along how Esau would take it. She called up Jacob, and whispered to him, 'Look, Esau hates you, and the only cheer he has is by planning to kill you. Now then, you fly down to my brother Laban, your uncle, and stay with him until Esau has cooled off. Then I'll send for you and you can come back.'

And so Jacob hot-footed it down to Haran, to his uncle Laban's place, to hide out.

Now may I remind you again, that it is not Jacob's story I'm bringing you to. It is the story of one of his sons that I am thinking about. But you can see now perhaps why any son of Jacob should have something of his background explained, because it is the sort of background that explains such a lot.

And I must tell you more still about Jacob. For although you can already see the twists and crookedness in his parents and in his home, you have still to appreciate the particular crookedness that he now proceeded to develop on his own! For what he had learnt from poor, insecure Isaac, and shrewd, crooked, unscrupulous Rebecca, was only a shadow alongside the solid blackness of wicked, treacherous Uncle Laban. Jacob is surely coming up through one of the toughest schools in all human history. And remember—remember well—Jacob is one of God's men. And so is Isaac, and so is Abraham. Never, never forget that God 'chooses' His people for a vastly greater and more unique reason than that of being nice. These are some of the most un-nice men ever to be found; but these three are all God's men.

Jacob arrived at Laban's property at mid-day, as a party of shepherds were coming to a well, to water their sheep. Jacob walked up, and introduced himself. Just then, along came one of Laban's daughters, Rachel.

'Then Jacob kissed Rachel.' There can be no doubt that it was a discreet and cousinly greeting. But I rather think Freud was well represented, as we shall see!

Rachel took the news home to Laban, and he welcomed Jacob warmly. The old scoundrel was no doubt already wondering how he could exploit his penniless nephew. And sure enough a month later his chance arrived. Laban said to Jacob, 'Look. Just because you are a kinsman, you shouldn't work for me for nothing. What would you like to have from me as wages?'

Now Laban had two daughters. The name of the elder was Leah, the younger was Rachel. And I am absolutely certain the old chiseller had been watching Jacob and Rachel, and Rachel and Jacob, and knew what was coming.

The old historian of this book of Genesis never wastes words. Writing then was not a matter of scribbling away with a satin-pointed pen, tap-tapping on a typewriter, or dictating into an electronic recording device. Writing was effort. And in cryptic, imaginative strokes, a world of information is given in a few words. 'Leah's eyes were weak.' I have often chuckled away at this masterpiece of descriptive brevity. Was it a squint that disfigured Leah? Did she have some cicatricial ectropion with possibly ugly, rolled-down eyelids? Was it some chronic inflammation, which made her perpetually red-eyed and unattractive? We will never know for sure. But in the four words, 'Leah had weak eyes', the writer has implied everything. And he settles the whole field of innuendo and imagination by the genius of adding: 'But Rachel was beautiful and lovely.'

And Jacob was head over heels in love with the beautiful and lovely Rachel; and probably hardly even noticed, except by an involuntary movement of recoil, the blear-eyed, red-eyed, wall-eyed, cross-eyed, 'weak-eyed' Leah.

Wages? Jacob leapt at his uncle's question. How to get lovely Rachel. Just the chance to turn that first cousinly kiss of welcome into the warm passionate embrace of husband and lover. 'I'll work for your younger daughter, Rachel. I'll work seven years for her.'

I must say this is one of the most delightful and

noble things ever recorded about any man. Jacob may
have been mixed up, and crooked, and a cheat. But in
his love, he is the real man. Laban had already sensed
this, and jumped at the offer. 'Might as well be you, as
some stranger,' he agreed non-committally, shrewdly
hiding his satisfaction. And this is what we read in the
case-notes that God has left us in the book of Genesis:
'So Jacob served seven years for Rachel, and they
seemed to him but a few days because of the love he
had for her.'

Jacob is in love. Madly, passionately in love. Probably for the first time in all his young life, he has begun
to feel the deep emotional security of being rated, of
being himself. He is working for Rachel. He is going
to be married, married to Rachel. 'You know Rachel,
don't you? She's that lovely, beautiful girl over there.
And she's not only the prettiest girl in the world, she's
a wonder with the flocks, and very nice to talk to, and
quick, and intelligent, and a great girl in the home,
and just the most gorgeous looking girl you ever saw,
and, and. . . . I am going to marry her. Yes. Only seven
years. . . .'

'Gee—it's only three years off. . . .'

'Gosh—next year I'm going to be married to Rachel.'

'Hey—wake up fellahs, it'll be dawn soon. And
today I'm getting married to Rachel. Aren't I just the
luckiest dog in the world? Rachel! Married to Rachel!
Hurrah, today—Rachel!'

Yes. It's the wedding day. The seven years were
nothing to Jacob, so long as he married lovely Rachel.
And the ceremony is in progress. It is one of those long-
drawn, oriental torture affairs. Apparently very like a
modern Western wedding. Guests and speeches and
toasts and all that sort of mumbo-jumbo by the hour.
Jacob is hardly with us, is he? He's in such a whirl of
ecstasy. He's just madly in love with her. It is just as
well the bride is veiled, or he'd be sure to blow a fuse,
or burst a blood vessel, or have a seizure or something.

But at last it's over. The day had dragged through,
and the magic incantations and all the bits and pieces

are over, and at last the bride and bridegroom are led to the special bridal tent that has been pitched for them. In the darkness of the night, but in the glow and passion of seven years of preparation, the marriage is consummated. Their first night together. Their wedding night. Jacob is with Rachel.

And as the sun's rays light the tent in the morning, Jacob wakes, and turns to gaze freely now at the lovely wife he has won. And there, staring at him across the sheets, is blear-eyed, red-eyed, wall-eyed, cross-eyed, 'weak-eyed' Leah! He has been tricked! He has been married to the elder, ugly sister. Laban has played the joker, and Jacob has lost.

What did I say before, about Laban? Did I say he was an old chiseller? Did I refer to him as a scoundrel? Did I suggest that he would be known as wicked, treacherous Uncle Laban? Yes, I did. And the chiselling, scoundrelly, wicked treachery of this wedding day is surely the dirtiest trick any uncle ever played on a tense, emotionally taut, unsuspecting nephew.

'Tut-tut,' said Uncle Laban, blandly, as hot words of protest formed on Jacob's trembling lips. 'My dear boy, don't be childish and silly. In our society it is always the eldest daughter who marries first. We are very respectable people. And we could never let our good name be spoiled by having a younger daughter married off first. But just another seven years, and Rachel is yours also. Yes, I'd be delighted to see you have both of my girls.' And off he went, looking very righteous, and tut-tutting his deep concern for the preservation of the decencies of the society, and correctness of all such procedures.

Jacob, you have been born into a tough family, and you had better get tough, or you'll go clean under.

And Jacob began to play it tough too. And he played it tougher and tougher; until in the end he clean licked old Laban at his own game!

He started by doing another seven years for Rachel. (Give old uncle his dues, he let the young man have her, as it were, on credit. Jacob was given Rachel the week after he married Leah; then had to work on for seven more years to pay back the mortgage, so to speak.)

Yes, Jacob. You had better learn to play this game tough. And Jacob is eager enough and happy enough, now, to play the man, and set out on the road of life as a husband and father. For of course he has Rachel as his wife now. And she will bear him sons, the greatest riches any man can own or know. Yes, of course, Rachel, his lovely wife, and her splendid sons.

And as the months went by, Rachel had no sons. She was not pregnant. But Leah was. Blear-eyed Leah had a son. And Jacob was only the more hurt. The son from Leah was no son to him. It was Leah who gave the baby the name Reuben.

Leah had another son; she called him Simeon. And another, Levi. And another, Judah. And Rachel was barren. If you can see Jacob as he should be seen, if you can understand his sad, complex personality as it should be understood, you can see the iron eating into his soul. Each son of Leah's is just so much salt rubbed into the wound of disappointment and emotional distress.

And now Rachel is upset. She is in tears. Tears of envy for Leah, self-pity for herself. No sons, and 'weak-eyed' Leah has four. But Rachel has a maid, Bilhah. She came to Jacob and asked him to take the slave maid as a concubine, and let Bilhah have children on behalf of Rachel. Anything rather than barrenness, rather than no sons at all.

In our intensely monogamous society, we look askance at this suggestion; and more still at its acceptance by Jacob. But that is again because we are so far removed in our culture from theirs, that the poignancy, the urgency of it escapes us. And Bilhah has two sons, Dan and Naphtali.

Then Leah did the same. She had a maid too, Zilpah. And Zilpah bore two sons to Jacob, Gad and Asher.

And now the whole family is caught up in this tense, bitter competition. There is a pitiful tale of the two wives bartering mandrakes, for the chance of pregnancy. Leah is despairing, because while she has sons, she has no husband—Jacob is not in love with her, or her sons. And Rachel is distraught, because she has his affections, but no sons to return.

And Leah has another son, Issachar; and a sixth, Zebulun (and a daughter, Dinah).

Ten sons, now. Six by Leah. Two each by each maid. And none that Jacob called his own; none of them sons of the only love in his love-starved life.

And then, wonder of wonders, delight of all delights —Rachel bore a son. Into this atrocious mess of social insecurity and conflicts comes baby Joseph. Number eleven in the list of sons. What a ghastly setting for any child to have to grow up in.

And now Jacob is happy. He has made it. He is a father. His wife is a mother, and it is time for him to leave Laban, and set out on his own, and make a home for his son. And we breathe a sigh of relief, for we see that now there is a chance for all these tangled threads to become sorted out; and for life to come to some better arrangement.

But if we think that, then we are miles off the mark. Jacob is tangled with Laban. And you don't just walk up to Laban and say: 'Well, goodbye, Uncle Laban. Thanks a million for all your help. How about a couple of hundred sheep and goats as a parting present?' No. Not with Laban. Certainly not. Jacob is learning how the game must be played if he wants to play among crooks like his mother's family.

'Uncle Laban,' he said. 'Don't you think I should leave you? I'll just take my wives and children—they are fully paid up, remember—and I'll be off.'

'Well, fancy your feeling like that, Jacob! Do you know, I've been doing a bit of thinking, and I've decided that God has been prospering me because of having you with me. Why not stay on, and work for me; and you just name your wages.'

It's real oriental bargaining. It's the real poker school.

'Ah, yes,' said Jacob, 'I know that too. I can see how much richer you've become since I started working for you. But how can I make enough for myself, and to provide for my own home and household that way?'

Laban is puzzled. He doesn't know what to say. He can't afford to lose Jacob, who is a master of the studs and of caring for the flocks. But if he doesn't want wages, make the young fellow show his hand.

'What do you want me to give you then, Jacob?'

'Oh, nothing, Uncle Laban. I don't want you to give me anything, but I've been thinking. What say from now on we cull out from the flocks all the black and speckled and spotted lambs and goats that are born and then let me have them? Then I'll stay on and work for you, but the black and spotted stock will become mine and of course all the prime quality and unmarked flocks are yours.'

'Good,' said Laban, after a moment's thought. His mind had been working like lightning and he could see in this a good scheme especially for himself. 'It's a deal.' And as they drank to the deal and went through the usual business palaver of one rogue outsmarting another rogue, Laban tipped off his sons and they raced through the flocks and gathered all the black and spotted and speckled and striped rams and ewes and took them off three days' journey away!

Jacob, didn't I tell you it's a tough school? This is not a class for beginners.

'No,' says Jacob, 'and I'm not a beginner. Look, I've been doing a bit of stud control. I've found that if I take rods of poplar and almond and plane trees and peel white stripes in the bark and expose them to the breeding flocks, then they breed striped and speckled lambs and kids. And even if cheating old Laban has stolen away all the marked rams and ewes, I'll get more to replace them. I'll be all right.'

Jacob, you are learning. What you are learning is very unsound genetics of course, and we smile today at this highly unscientific explanation. But you are learning to out-cheat the cheats and even to out-Laban

Laban. And, Jacob, that is really saying something.

Joseph, baby Joseph, you see the sort of household you have arrived in? Why, I notice that you are wearing some sort of fancy dress. What is that for, Jacob? What is this strange cloak little Joseph is toddling around in? Reuben and Simeon and Judah and Levi never had a cloak like this. Theirs were all short boyish cloaks with short sleeves.

'Ah, yes,' replies Jacob. 'That's the special long-sleeved cloak of the eldest son. He is Rachel's firstborn, my eldest son—I do hope she can have some more boys still. But at least I've got Joseph.'

And Jacob goes out proudly remembering this eleventh son as his eldest, and cuts more stripes in the bark of almond and poplar sticks to breed more ring-straked cattle and flocks.

Yes, this is Joseph. This is the man we have been coming to study. We have had to include in our understanding all this background of trickery and intrigue and home bitterness and jealousy, because God Himself has included it all in His own official record. This is the origin and setting of Joseph, one of God's men. This is the raw material of a life in which God is now going to work. Here is a life that has so many complexes and high spots of distortion that you can never miss seeing what happens. Joseph will teach you, as clearly as in any case ever recorded, just what is likely to happen to you if you really set out to put your life in God's hands.

But, you may ask, what about Rachel, lovely Rachel? She may not be like the others. Grandfather Isaac, grandmother Rebecca, grandfather Laban (for he is grandpa to little Joseph) and father Jacob may be a pretty quaint bunch. But Rachel may be the one to straighten the boy out. She may have a better integration of personality, she may have had a simple, reliable, emotionally rich mother, to give her true love and security. Yes, that's it. Rachel will have the answer.

God is very fair and straight in what He tells us in

His Textbook. He doesn't ever need the help of men
or women, and He has recorded another little incident
which will for ever stop us making that sort of mistake. It is a single incident, but it is enough. Sordid,
mean, miserable, embarrassing. This time it is about
Rachel.

Jacob had obviously achieved a genetic mutation, at
least a genetic variant in the flocks and herds. He was
over three thousand years ahead of Mendel and Darwin,
but he was producing in the flocks a larger and larger
proportion of spotted and speckled animals. And the
time arrived when his striped beasts outnumbered
Laban's un-striped. And Jacob could see the growing
annoyance and finally the hatred in the face of Laban.
Jacob is not a big man, not really big enough to go up
to Laban and have it settled as man to man. He decided to collect his stock and his family and just sneak
off. He told his two wives, and together they planned
to decamp while Laban was away shearing.

The plan worked splendidly. 'And Jacob outwitted
Laban the Aramean, in that he did not tell him that
he intended to flee. He fled with all that he had, and
arose and crossed the Euphrates.'

That seems fair enough, of course. Jacob took only
the flocks and herds that were strictly his own. Yes, he
did. But 'Rachel stole her father's household gods'.
Only six words. And what a wealth of implication and
innuendo! 'Now Jacob did not know that Rachel had
stolen them.'

When Laban came home, he was furious. He set out
hot foot after Jacob in a rage that would not be quelled
until his precious gods were back in his hands. Household gods to Laban, as to all the human Labans after
him, have been the really important things in life. Why,
I have seen a surgeon in the foulest of tempers because
he was delayed in an operating theatre one morning,
when it was his afternoon for golf. I have known a
church committee meeting postponed because the time
of meeting clashed with one of the favourite radio-
serials one of the churchwardens was following. Here,

in Australia, time and time again we have seen the
whole economy of a branch of industry, and even of
the State, modified to make it possible for shift-workers
to get their pot of beer after work. Yes, household gods,
whether gold images or chromium T.V. sets, have
always been very serious and important. 'And Rachel
stole her father's household gods.' Lovely Rachel!
Dear, sweet Rachel!

Laban was livid. For a full week he had tracked after
his son-in-law, finally catching up with him away in
the Gilead hills. As he rode into Jacob's camp he was
already almost speechless. 'What are you sneaking away
for, Jacob? If you want to go, why don't you do it
openly and honourably? Aren't your wives my own
daughters? Aren't your children my grandchildren?
Why just sneak off like a guilty man? Yes, Jacob, like
a guilty man. And, Jacob'—I can almost hear the icy
bite in his voice now as he speaks in tense, quiet, bitter
tones—'why did you steal my household gods?'

Jacob couldn't miss the point, and didn't. He doesn't
know a thing about the stolen gods, but he sees how
serious this charge is. He knows that simply decamping
with his flocks and family is fair enough—Laban would
never have hesitated to do the same. But household
gods are really a different matter altogether. Jacob
flushed with anger and flared back his reply. 'I left you
like that because I couldn't trust you! You have
cheated me all along the line, and I know you would
still like to cheat me out of my wives. But I haven't
touched your gods, or anything else that is really yours.
And if you find your gods I'll kill the person who took
them. You just hunt around, and see if you can find
them. Go on, start looking!'

Did you hear that, Rachel? Pretty Rachel, that's you
Jacob is talking about. What will you do now, Rachel,
with those gods tucked away in the saddle bags of the
camel you were riding? Watch the feverish way your
dad is scouring around in the tents and among all the
goods, looking for his precious gods. Look out, Rachel,
lovely Rachel, he's coming to ask you to give him a

hand in his search; and no doubt to check up on you too. And Rachel smiled up at her father ever so sweetly, and in the most butter-won't-melt-in-her-mouth tones said, 'Oh, Daddy dear, I would like to help you all I can. But I know you won't be annoyed with me if I don't get up.' And here she turned her head aside shyly and blushed ever so prettily, as with long lashes drooped over her lovely eyes she half-whispered, 'You know how it is with us women, Daddy. It's just one of those times.'

Baby Joseph, you see that pretty lady there sitting in the saddle in the tent? That girl who can cheat and lie so prettily and so delightfully that even her own father is deceived by her? Joseph, that's your mother. She is the one you are going to share, with your cunning father, in your critical formative boyhood years.

Yes indeed, Joseph will teach us, perhaps as no other story ever told could teach us, that God accepts, as raw material, men who in our social judgment would be very unacceptable. But we shall be learning that God has never even hinted that His idea for men is that they should be chosen just because they are nice polished gentlemen with good manners and a nice home life. And let us be quite frank. It's just as well for us that that is not His idea for us, or none of us would make the grade. We didn't have Jacob for a father or Rachel for a mother; but perhaps the poor, repellent young Teddy Boy round the corner in the magistrates' court did. And that objectionable delinquent kid you read about on the front page of last night's paper— perhaps he had a big serious dominant father like Abraham. Yes, we were spared that too. We are just normal fellows, aren't we? Sure, we are as normal as you like.

But wait a moment. If we are quite honest with ourselves, doesn't that make us admit that we have the same conflicts and repressions and insecurities and over-compensations and all the rest of it that Joseph had, but not so marked?

Yes, Joseph teaches us that lesson, and teaches it for

all time. If he is one of God's men it is not because he is nice, any more than he could be one of God's men because he is *not* nice. For Joseph is certainly not nice. How could he be? Petted and pampered and spoilt as perhaps no child has ever been before or since, he is absolutely insufferable. He is the most objectionable young prig that ever strutted around in a long-sleeved gown.

And as if all this background isn't enough, while he is just a lad, his mother had another son and died in childbirth. Joseph is now motherless. And into *his* life is now poured all the over-stressed affection his father had felt for Rachel. He is made the property manager, and is at home with his father administering the new property they are occupying, while the ten elder brothers are out in the fields. How they hated him. And how well they might hate him.

The historian recording this tragic tale has recorded three episodes to give us our proper perspective on the family set up. Joseph is just coming to manhood. He is seventeen now; a youth to us, but in their day and race a young man. And the writer first records baldly that Joseph was out in the fields with the sons of Bilhah and Zilpah, and came home and split on them. Never mind what it was all about—the important thing is that he has reached manhood and is still a tale-teller. And Dad lapped it up. The brothers hated Joseph.

Then again, one day the family were all sitting down to breakfast at the long, family table. Dad up one end, Joseph (now that mother had died) up the other. Joseph rapped on the table. 'Listen, you chaps, I'll tell you a dream I had last night.'

From the other end of the table came Jacob's stern old voice—'Listen, boys. Listen to what Joseph has to say.'

There followed that strained silence that comes over the class when a hated headmaster comes in—the caricature of obedience that is mere compulsion.

'Yes, wait till I tell you my dream. I dreamed we

were all out in the field binding sheaves of wheat,
when suddenly my sheaf stood up on end, and then all
your sheaves gathered around and bowed down to
mine. Wasn't that a wonderful dream?'

Poor young Joseph. He is so utterly spoiled and so
entirely smug that he doesn't hear the murmured words
of hatred. '. . . rule over us . . .' '. . . boss over us
already, what does he want now?' '. . . him and his
lousy dreams.'

Poor young Joseph—you don't see it, do you? You
can't hear them, can you? No, it's a great gag, isn't it?
That was a wonderful dream. Pity you can't have
another like it, Joseph, and put the elder brothers
really in their place.

'Oh yes, but I can, though. Listen, boys, while I tell
you another dream. This one is a real whizzer.'

Yes, this was a wonderful dream. 'I dreamed I saw
the sun and the moon and eleven stars all bowing down
to me. Gee, it was a wonderful dream. I wish you could
all have seen it.'

Jacob looked up sternly, in rebuke. 'What do you
mean, son? What sort of a dream is that? Do you suggest that your late mother and I and your brothers will
all come to bow down to you?' And the old man looked
rather vaguely at Joseph, and that was all.

The brothers all sat there, tense, fuming. Think
what would have happened to Reuben if he had said
that. Think of the trouble Dan and Naphtali, Gad and
Asher, the sons of Bilhah and Zilpah would have been
in if they had told a dream like that. Deep, burning,
jealous hatred was scorching them through and through.

This then is Joseph, the young man Joseph, the man
God was to accept as one of His own; this is the raw
material God accepts in a man of faith. Not because
complexes and insecurities and human failures are
attractive to God, but because faith, that rare, precious
thing which is faith, is the only thing which God seeks
in a man. All the other things He can make, if the
man He is to make them in is a man of faith.

And now we are off on the story of how God set

about doing just this. Of how God took Joseph, hated, priggish, conceited, spoilt-brat Joseph, and began re-making him, re-creating him, making him 'new-born' as Jesus once described this process. Come with me and watch.

The first move was very simple. It consisted merely in Jacob sending the ten elder brothers away into a rather distant part, to pasture their father's flocks. Joseph of course was kept at home. The eldest son must be around the homestead to be with Dad.

But then Jacob began to wonder how they were get-ting on over in Shechem. 'Joseph, go and find out,' he said one day, as his imagination set him wondering about the ten eldest. 'Go and see how your brothers are making out. Check up on the flocks. I'd like a bit of news.'

So Joseph set off for Shechem, only to find they had moved on to Dothan. He set out for Dothan. As he came walking over the hills his brothers saw him com-ing. They couldn't miss seeing him, dressed in his long-sleeved gown.

I don't know, but I think I am right in guessing that a lot of their talk together, while they had been away from home, had been about Joseph. For as he appeared on the skyline they all burst out in clamorous hate: 'Ha! Here comes the dreamer!' 'So it is. Now's our chance. Let's kill him.' 'Yes, and we will pitch him in one of the pits, and he will never be found.' 'Why not say a wild animal has killed him?' 'That's the idea! That'll settle his dreams.'

'Hey, Reuben! What do you think of that? What say we kill the hateful little dreamer and get rid of him for keeps?'

Yes, Reuben, what do you think of that? You are middle-aged. You are the eldest. You should be wear-ing that long-sleeved cloak, not that little swank Joseph. What do you say?

Reuben is tight-lipped. He hates Joseph as much as any of them, and with more reason. But he doesn't like

to see the boy killed. 'No,' he said flatly. 'I won't ha
any actual bloodshed. Let's just pitch him into one of
the old, dry wells, and not kill him in cold blood.'
Reuben was thinking that a few hours of that would
teach the little blighter a whole lot of good; and then
he would sneak back at night and hook him out again.
'No, don't kill him. But into the pit with him.'

Joseph has no more idea of what is going on than
you would expect in any eleventh son who has had the
disastrous misfortune to be treated and trusted by his
father as the eldest. The swaggering arrival is in so
few searing seconds turned to utter disaster. Off came
the hated long-sleeved gown. Down he went into the
pit-bottom. Down into the desolation which no sobbing
and tears could ever hope to relieve.

What a luncheon-party it was. For the ten men at the
top it was the best lunch they had eaten for years—no
more dreams with meals, no more telling tales to Dad,
no more Joseph. And for the youngster at the bottom—
the unspeakable terror and bitterness of all his world
shattered and torn away from him in one searing
minute. Can't you see the white face and eyes staring
up at his brothers as they sit munching their cheese
and egg sandwiches, throwing him the burned bits of
crust with jeers and taunts?

Joseph, you are one of God's men. You are a man of
faith. Has God forgotten you? Do you think He has any
ideas for you?

Joseph, God has not forgotten you. This is not an
oversight on His part. This is not jealous and envious
brothers tricking God into a defensive counter-move.
No, Joseph, this is the way God is taking you and in
His measureless skill and endless love beginning to re-
make you. Look, Joseph, God has already been planning, and the plan is now unfolding. You can't see
from down there in the bottom of the well, but coming
over the hill-top towards the north-east is a caravan—
a group of Arab traders, and they are God's next move
for you.

The elder brothers saw the Arabs too, of course.

There was the camel train bearing right down on them. Judah was the one who hit on the bright idea. 'Listen, fellows. Here's an idea. Why not sell the young rat to the Arabs? That will give us some very nice jingly pocket money, and then we won't be guilty of killing him. After all, he is our dear half-brother. What do you say?'

And of course they said yes! To be paid cash and at the same time square their conscience—why, of course! 'Come on, Joseph. You can come up now. Grab hold of this rope.'

Joseph, did you think your brothers had learned to like you, and were bringing you up to be friends? Then you don't know them for what they are. They don't like you, because you like yourself too much. But Joseph, God Himself loves you. And now you are well on the way, in His great hands of love, to something unspeakably good and great.

'Twenty silver shekels. Thanks a lot for calling in, Dreamer. Our Arab cousins have paid us that for you. Now you can run along with them and tell them your dreams. Tell them how the sun and the moon and the stars all bow down to you, Dream-boy! They'll laugh their heads off, won't they? This is the best day's business we have ever had. Twenty silver shekels *and* rid of you. So long, Joseph, sweet dreams. . . .'

Joseph, you are on your way to Egypt. On your way to slavery. . . .

Joseph, you are up for sale. That is you that tubby-looking Egyptian guards officer is chattering about with your Arab captors. That is Captain Potiphar, and he has bought you. You are his slave.

Joseph, how does it feel to be a slave? Remember the long-sleeved gown you used to wear? Yes, I know, Joseph—you will never be able to forget it—and that is one of the things that makes it feel so bad, isn't it? That rough shapeless thing you are wearing is only a 'garment'—you couldn't really give it any proper descriptive name, could you? Slaves don't wear gowns, or suits, or coats, do they? Just 'garments'. One last question, Joseph—you are one of God's men of faith. Tell me this—has He forgotten you? Is He still with you?

When our English Bible was first being translated, one of the loveliest statements ever made was made at this very point in the story. In the 'Great' Bible, and in the 'Breeches' Bible, the translators, in their new-found English version, translated the answer to this question like this: 'The Lord was with Joseph, and he was a lucky fellow.'

Yes, there he is, the lucky fellow. All the luck in the world—and all the luck in heaven too. God is with him, and that is why he is so lucky. That is the only thing that can ever make a man say he is lucky. Yes, that alert-looking, handsome young Hebrew, wearing the 'garment' of a slave; that fellow who has just lost his father and his home and his family and his fortune—he's the lucky one. God is with him, and God is looking after him, in the way He always looks after His men. And His care of Joseph has just shown itself by getting the young man sold into slavery.

Can you understand this? Never mind if you can't. Joseph didn't either. I don't think he understood it for another fifty years. But perhaps we shall be able to understand it with him as we read on.

Joseph is a slave (the lucky fellow!) in Potiphar's house. And while he may have been a prig and conceited pup, he was none the less efficient, capable, reliable. Potiphar soon found that he was a man to be trusted, and made him overseer in his whole household. In fact Joseph came to handle Potiphar's affairs so effectively that the old Hebrew historian writes about Potiphar by saying that 'he left all that he had in Joseph's charge, and having him he had no concern for anything but the food which he ate'.

No doubt Potiphar thought how lucky he was! He could now spend all his time playing darts down in 'The Memphis Arms', or enjoying whatever equivalent pleasure came to the lot of the fortunate guards officer who had Joseph at home. And, no doubt also, Potiphar would tell his fellow officers all about this gem of a slave he had picked up—'You know, when he came to me he didn't know a word of Egyptian—only spoke his own heathenish lingo—and now I can leave every single thing in his care. All I have to do is feed myself!' And Potiphar would pat his now rather noticeable paunch and order a last round of drinks before toddling back home to his pretty young wife.

And Mrs. Potiphar, what do you think of it all? How do you feel, having a handsome young slave round all day, while Captain Potiphar is away on duty? Yes, Mrs. Potiphar, what do you think of him? You've been watching him, following him around all the morning, haven't you? And all day yesterday too, and the day before, and for days and days before that? Mrs. Potiphar, what are you looking so coy about? That's your very prettiest new dress, and those are your finest jewels—shouldn't you keep them for special occasions? And that's the most expensive scent you have been using, and altogether, Mrs. Potiphar, you look like an excited adolescent waiting to go out on a special date with her most particular boy-friend!

Joseph, have you noticed Mrs. Potiphar? She has never been more than a step or two away from you since she kissed her husband goodbye at the front door this morning. Did you notice the slight tremble in her hand as she gave you your list of tasks for the day? Did you hear the slight huskiness in her voice as she went over the day's accounts with you? And she is saying something to you again now, Joseph. She is half-whispering, perhaps that's why you didn't quite seem to catch on. Is that why, Joseph? She is saying it again—listen—'Joseph, give me a kiss. Joseph'—and she has dropped her long dark lashes over her deep flashing eyes, and with the blazing colour in her cheeks she does look adorable, doesn't she?—'Joseph'—and she has taken your hands in hers now, as she stands right beside you, looking up into your handsome young face, whispering softly—'Come up to my room with me, lie down with me. I want to be your lover. . . .'

Joseph stepped back, bewildered, distressed. 'But

Mrs. Potiphar, I couldn't. Captain Potiphar has left me entirely free to look after every single thing he possesses except you, for you are his wife. Oh, Mrs. Potiphar, please don't talk like that. That is a terrible thing to say, and how could I face your husband if I agreed? How could I face God?'

And Joseph slipped away quickly, to get on with his work, glad at last to hear the heavy step and hearty guffaws of his master. Thank goodness he's home. I hope it doesn't happen again. I can remember the awful sick look on Dad's face when he heard about Reuben and Bilhah—and she was only a concubine. And all the row in the family over Dinah and Hamar, even though they got properly married. And Judah and Tamar. These are things a man should be very careful about, marriage is so important in the will of God. I do hope she will forget all about me.

Joseph, God is with you, you lucky fellow. You are one of His men, and He has the whole situation under control. He knows all about Mrs. Potiphar. His mind is great enough to know every complicated neuronic reaction in her cerebral cortex, every microgramme of circulating hormone, every insecurity reaction in her behaviour pattern.

God knows that tomorrow she will feel just the same, that she will be even more urgent in her soliciting. God can hear her—as she whispers and asks day after day, now, doesn't she, Joseph? 'Joseph, a kiss. Joseph, don't you love me just a little bit? Come up to my room, Joseph, we can be alone there.'

Yes, God hears all this, and in the greatness of His mind He knows it all even before it has come into the time-space manifestation that we call the 'now' of human experience.

Joseph, God knows all about today, too. This is going to be a momentous day for you. He is with you, you lucky fellow. You are today still bound and carried in His 'steadfast love'.

Yes, it was a very particular day for Joseph. The days had become rather monotonously alike lately—every day a day for Mrs. Potiphar to come appealing, calling, entreating, seducing. But today all the other slaves are outside, and only the two of them are in the house. Poor Madam, in her now obsessional emotion, sees her chance. She seized Joseph in her passionate embrace, pressing her warm trembling body against his. 'Oh, Joseph! Please! Come on, take me. You must, please.'

Joseph is trapped. She has him held in the fierce passionate embrace of a desperate emotionally distraught greed. With a sudden quick turn and a wrench Joseph fled, her long nails tearing red furrows across his shoulders as he escaped, his shapeless slave's garment dragged off him by her wild clutches.

Naked and in pain Joseph darted out of the house. Anything to be free of Potiphar's wife.

What did Mrs. Potiphar do? What would you expect her to do? Slaves are to her just merchandise, chattels. It is probably inconceivable to her that a slave should resist such attentions and commands, as she had been making. To be disobeyed, worse still to be scorned in her womanhood, is bitterest gall. The passion of appeal turned to the fury of hate.

She called in the men of her household, and white with rage, frustration, self-pity, she burst out her story. 'Look—he has brought among us a Hebrew to insult us. He came in to rape me, and I screamed at the top of my voice. When he heard me yelling he dashed out of the house, and left his garment behind. Look—here it is.'

As Captain Potiphar came home that evening, humming lightly the latest saucy tap-room jingle he had heard that day, he was barely in the front gate before the story poured out.

Poor Potiphar. I am quite sure he never understood what it was really all about. The innuendo, the emotional overtones, of his wife's opening outburst— 'The Hebrew servant, whom you brought among us . . .' are lost to him. All he can see is the slave trying to seduce and rape his pretty wife. He can't see the hidden bitterness and reproach she is showing for him.

Potiphar is far too smug and unimaginative for that.
He just flared up in the silly way men like that do flare
up. 'His anger was kindled. And Joseph's master took
him and put him into the prison, the place where the
king's prisoners were confined, and he was there in
prison.'

Hello, Joseph. I see you are in prison now. Surely it
was bad enough to lose your family and your home and
your wealth and your freedom. But to be in prison—
and in the king's prison, too—that is the dead end,
surely. God must have forgotten you. This must be
some slip-up on His part. Joseph, tell me, what do you
think God has been doing about it?

I don't know what Joseph thought; and I am quite
sure that whatever it was, he could not have told me,
as the shaking sobs burst from his trembling lips. That
young man with the white, drawn face isn't in a fit
state to tell us anything at all, except that he is in
trouble, and in it clean up to his neck. And never
never never, if you could get any clear answer from him
there in prison, would he have told you he thought this
was the good thing, the lucky thing. But it was. 'The
Lord was with Joseph and showed him steadfast love.'

Do you think this hard to understand? To understand
how the steadfast love of God is so big a thing, so
strong, so good in its intention, that it can override our
human love of comfort and convenience like this? Of
course you do; and so did Joseph, and so does every
saint of God in all history.

Joseph is in prison. He is just the age when he should
be thinking about marriage; and getting his home set
up; and securing his career; and all that. . . .

In his twenties now. . . . Middle twenties. . . . Later
twenties. . . . His old distress about losing his father
and home are now away in the past, time-healed, no
doubt. But jail is just deadly in its endless getting
nowhere. Each day like the day before. Each year like
last year, except that it makes the leaden heaviness
seem heavier. It is now this deadly crushing dullness
all the time. It was hard to stand the shocks of his

brothers' hatred, of being whisked away into slavery, of being seduced by Mrs. Potiphar, of being pitched into prison. Those happenings nearly beat the heart out of him, Joseph would admit. But this deadly grinding at a timeless mill is the real killer. This is where the iron eats into the soul of a man.

Joseph has the thing organized, of course. He is just about the world's champion organizer, and is in charge of the whole dungeon-full of prisoners. The gaolers can now do what Potiphar did—leave it to Joseph.

And so year rolls after year, and all the early prime of young life has been wasted away for ever. We read the story in a few words in the book of Genesis, and pass it off as though there were nothing to it. But to the man who has to go through it all, this is not a story where you can skip through the nasty bits and forget all about it a moment later. This is slow deadly murder.

I have sometimes tried to speculate about Joseph's thoughts and hopes and prayers during these long years. But it is only speculation. Those years are between Joseph and God. What God was saying to the young man, how he thought it was affecting him at the time, we are not to know—we are not told. But that it did affect him—yes, that is the thing we are to know. That is the thing that God wants us to see very clearly indeed, for that is the thing He is doing in all His men. (And does that now involve you and me?)

Sometimes the drudging monotony of the prison would be lifted somewhat. One day there was quite a stir when two newcomers landed down in the cells. One was the king's own personal butler; the other the king's baker. They had done something to annoy the Pharaoh, who had them tossed into jail, where they came under Joseph's care.[1]

[1] The odd thing about all this is that while Joseph was in charge of them, it is still recorded that 'he waited on them'. To anyone who knows the New Testament, and knows the Greater-than-Joseph of the Gospels, this is one of those sparkling jewels in the Old Writings, flashing out the light concerning the One who, though so rich, became the poorest bond-slave, willing even to wash the hands and feet of His followers.

And then one day there was another slight change from the tedium of prison life. The butler and the baker had been dreaming, and were recounting their dreams.

The butler told his dream first. He had dreamed of a vine with three branches. And in the dream he saw it bud into flower, and clusters of grapes form on the branches. And, bless his soul, he had Pharaoh's goblet in his hand, so he squeezed the juice from the grapes into the king's cup, and placed it in the king's own hand! 'That was a funny sort of dream, wasn't it? It has been bothering me ever since. What on earth do you think it means?' You may be certain that the butler was worried about it. A single gesture by the king had reduced him from king's cup-bearer to convict; and another such gesture could reduce him from convict to corpse! A most disturbing dream indeed!

'Say, Joseph. Do you know anything about dreams? What do you think it means?'

Joseph, dreams? My word, Joseph knows about dreams all right! It was dreams that had landed him in this pestilential dog-house of a prison. If they had been advertising in the 'Memphis Daily Times' for a Senior Lecturer in Dreams at Thebes University, he would have qualified for the job hands down.

His eyes were flashing as he burst out his answer. 'Yes, I'll tell you what your dream means. The three branches are three days. And in three days Pharaoh will elevate you again and take you out of this hole and re-instate you in your office. You will be back to your old job of king's butler. But listen'—and here I can see the eager excited gaze, as he clutched the butler's arm—'don't forget me, will you, when you are back in office? Please be kind enough to tell Pharaoh of my case, and get me out of here. I was stolen out of the Hebrew country and haven't done anything to warrant putting me in this dungeon.'

The baker watched this short drama with new interest. Dreams to him no doubt always told of trouble; but this sounded too good to let pass. 'Hey, listen, son. I had a dream too. I had three cake baskets on my head, and in the top basket were all sorts of food I had baked for Pharaoh. But all the birds kept eating the food out of the basket. What do you reckon that might mean?'

Joseph looked at him coldly, and rolled off his answer in the dispassionate manner of one who has seen it happen often enough. 'Sure, I'll tell you what it means, baker. But I don't too much like it, I tell you. The three baskets are three days; and in three days Pharaoh will elevate you too, but he'll do it by your head, and hang you on a tree. And it's you that the birds will be eating. Sounds bad to me, I'm afraid.'

Yes, that was a rather more interesting day; a couple of dreams can be enough to break the dull monotony, and give the prisoners something to joke and speculate about.

But sure enough, three days later, it happened. It was the king's birthday, and he had a party. I don't know what happened at the party, but I rather suspect that he got served Chablis with the roast, or Port with the fish, or something like that. But whatever it was, he remembered his butler. 'Where's that fellow Jeeves? Where's my proper butler? In jail? Then fetch him up. He shouldn't be in jail—the best butler I ever had! Of course I don't mean him to stay in prison. The clumsy oaf slopped a jug of claret over my new gold-braided cloak! A few weeks in jail is just the thing to teach him to be careful. And . . . Oh yes! There was that miserable baker! Cooked me a cake that was just solid dough in the middle and gave me indigestion for days. He's there too. Bring him up and hang him. An incompetent fool. I won't have a fellow like that around the palace. Go on! Do what I say. Hurry!'

What an exciting day that was. Especially for Joseph. As he saw the two prisoners go up the stairs, saw the wild excitement glowing delightedly in the face of the butler, the ashen despair of the baker, his pulse was racing, his mind seething with hope and confidence. He can't tear himself away from the gate through

130 PAGES FROM GOD'S CASE-BOOK

which he had called his last reminder to the butler to
do something for him . . .

He's been gone nearly an hour now. He must have
had time to get back to his buttling, time to say just a
word to Pharaoh about the unfortunate but very gifted
young Hebrew slave. . . . Perhaps he's waiting for a
really favourable chance. Perhaps it's not just as easy
as all that to get a word in with the king, while he's
eating and drinking. . . . Fancy, it's nearly dark—he
must be waiting for the evening banquet. . . . Perhaps
I'll have to wait until tomorrow . . . or tomorrow . . .
or . . . Oh no! It couldn't be! Surely not! He couldn't
have forgotten me. Not just forgotten. . . . Oh, no!

When I was a boy I used to like the story of Joseph.
I used to think what fun it must have been to be
Joseph—all those adventures and the big success story
it all turned into. Now that I am much older and have
spent a good many years working with people and so
often with people in trouble, this story about Joseph
has lost all that fun-and-adventure touch. When I now
come to this part where Joseph is just forgotten—
forgotten even by the lucky butler who was so glad to
have his head still on his shoulders that he could just
forget Joseph—then I must confess it puts quite a lump
in my throat, and I am not ashamed to admit that I
take off my slightly misty bifocals and give them a
good polishing. Because this seems to me to be the part
of the story that is nearly impossible to follow. Couldn't
God have made the butler remember Joseph? Of
course He could. Then did God intend deliberately
that Joseph was to be left there day after day, month
after month, two long tragic further years, before He
would make another move?

Yes, this is the way God does it. This is His plan in
love. The truth of the matter is that God is the only
One who does remember Joseph. Jacob remembers him
only to mourn for him. His brothers remember him
only to chuckle quietly (when Dad can't hear them)
and refer occasionally to 'twenty pieces of silver' as if
it were a family joke. Potiphar remembers him only

because he now has to try to look after his own affairs.
Mrs. Potiphar remembers him only in the growing
bitterness of dislike for Captain Potiphar. And the
butler doesn't remember him at all.

But God remembers him, every day, all the day.
'God was with him, showing him steadfast love.' Let
us go on, seeing His love at work.

This is Joseph's story. If you read it again in the
book of Genesis, remember that this is the history of
God and Joseph. There is a bit of Jacob in it, and a bit
of Potiphar, and a bit of this one and that one. But
it is theirs only because they are themselves in Joseph's
story.

And now there is a bit of Pharaoh in it again. Quite
a bit, and this is the light comic bit. This is the sun-
shine that clears away the cloud, the smile that dries
up the tears. This must make you smile, because
Pharaoh is really such a comical little fellow. You can't
for a moment think of this Pharaoh as being a big
stern giant of a potentate, measuring himself out in
history for a sphinx or a pyramid. Nothing like it. He
is the size Pharaoh who pops butlers and bakers into
prison and pops them out again.

And Pharaoh is now given the centre of the stage, as
he plays his little 'bit' part. Pharaoh has a dream!
Don't be surprised. It doesn't take a high I.Q. to have
a dream, so there is no surprise in Pharaoh having one.
And God, who designed the human cerebral cortex,
understood all about dreams long before Freud and
psychoanalysts started calling it Psychology and
Modern Knowledge. God is as well prepared to use
dreams to work out His steadfast love as He has been
to use jails and slave garments and forgetting butlers.

Pharaoh had a dream. It worried him, because he
couldn't understand it. No doubt he held all sorts of
doctorates from all sorts of seats of learning, but I am
sure they were very honorary. Any *summa cum laude*
or *ex honoris causa* in the citations was included for
the sake of politics rather than for intellect. And rack
his little brain as he would, he couldn't make out what

this dream meant. And neither could his court psycho
logists and his wise men. They were all stuck. The
dream was a puzzler, and they couldn't make head or
tail of it.

And then he remembered! The butler did! Hurrah!
The butler remembered Joseph! After two years, two
long dreadful hopeless years, he remembered. Out
poured the story of his faults, the story of the Hebrew
slave who was in jail with him and who could give the
interpretation of dreams.

Send for Joseph! Where is he? Is he still in prison?
Of course he is. God has been keeping him there, all
these years, showing him His steadfast love, beginning
to give to Joseph something that no Jacob, no Pharaoh,
could possibly give.

And Joseph is tubbed and scrubbed and clothed and
whisked up to Pharaoh. Pharaoh eyed the man. 'I have
had a dream, and they tell me you can interpret
dreams.'

'No sir. It's not something I can do myself, but God
will give Your Majesty a favourable answer.'

I am sure this was altogether too philosophical for
Pharaoh, but that didn't put him off. 'Listen then. I
dreamed I was standing on the banks of the Nile, when
some sleek fat cows came up out of the river and began
to eat the reed grass. Then seven gaunt scraggy cows,
such as I have never seen in Egypt, came up after them
and the thin cows ate up the fat cows; but they weren't
a scrap less gaunt for doing it.

'Then I went to sleep again, and dreamed I saw
seven ears of full rich grain growing on a stalk. And
seven thin, withered ears, blighted by the desert winds,
sprouted after them. And the seven thin ears swallowed
up the seven good ears. I have told my court magicians
over and over again, and there's not one of them who
can explain it to me.'

I may be unfair to Pharaoh, but I am sure he was
nearly in tears as he finished his little speech. It was
such a worrying dream. And as Joseph began to reply
I can see the puckered lips widen into a smile of sheer

delight—as with a child of any age who has at last got his longed-for little toy safely in his hands.

'The two dreams are really the same thing,' said Joseph. 'God has shown Your Majesty what He is going to do. The seven fat cows and the seven good ears are the same—they are seven years of great plenty in all Egypt. The seven lean cows and the seven withered ears of grain are also seven years, this time years of famine which will follow the seven rich years throughout the whole country. Then all the plenty of the seven rich years will be consumed in the famine. And the fact that the dream is repeated simply means that it is certain, and coming very soon.

'Now, Your Majesty . . .' And I can see all those years of organizing just oozing out of Joseph as he looks into the puzzled eyes of the pathetic little king. To the man who organized his ten elder brothers, who had organized Potiphar's whole affairs, who had organized the dungeons, Pharaoh was a push-over. 'Sir,' he went on; 'the thing to do is to pick out a man of great discretion and wisdom, and set him over the whole of Egypt. Then, sir, proceed to appoint overseers in the land, and levy a twenty per cent tax during the seven good years. Get these men to store up food and grain, backed by your personal authority, so that during the seven years of plenty they will build up huge reserves against the seven years of famine. That is the way to save the land. Now, sir, all you need to do is to find the right man, and your nation will be safe. Egypt will be able to come through the famine without trouble.'

The king was thoroughly impressed, as were his courtiers. 'That sounds wonderful,' said Pharaoh. 'But where can I find such a man as you speak of? A man like that would need to have a divine spirit, surely.' Poor little Pharaoh: he is himself supposed to be divine, but he is just intelligent enough to realize that it is utterly beyond his capacity to do it himself (and hasn't Joseph said as much, in any case?). 'Now where can I find a man like that?'

He looks at Joseph, for further help. And looks

again, as something flashes into his mind. 'Why, of course! If your God can tell you all this, then you must be just the man! You must be the wisest and most astute man there is. Listen!' Pharaoh raps for official attention. 'Here, then! I now appoint you to be in charge of all my people, and they must do just what you tell them. Only, but of course . . . that is . . . only I'm still on the throne, you know, I'm not included with them, don't you see?'

Joseph could see. He knew just what to do and how to do it. After nearly half his life spent in slavery and jail Joseph knew what was the right expression of grateful pleasure, the right touch of servility; but still the proper air of confidence and strength.

What a yarn! What a man! Only half an hour ago down in the dungeons. And now he is holding out his right hand, as Pharaoh announces: 'Take note! I hereby set you in charge of the whole of Egypt!' And Pharaoh takes the royal signet ring off his own hand and slips it on to Joseph's hand. Fine linen is called for; a gold chain about his neck; and (shades of Hans Andersen, A. A. Milne and all such story-tellers!) I can scarce forbear to burst out laughing as I hear the funny little king order out the second chariot and command that it be kept for Joseph. I can almost hear his simple mind saying, 'Now let me see. . . . I don't like to let him have the *Rolls*. . . . But he must at least have the *Cadillac*. . . . Yes. The second chariot. And a couple of postillions to call out "Bow the knee!" as he drives through the city. . . . But I really couldn't let him drive my lovely shining new *Rolls*.'

And Joseph was given a nice proper Egyptian name, Zaphenath-paneah; and he was given a nice little wife of very very good family. Joseph (do you mind if I still call him that?) has at last arrived.

'And Joseph was thirty years old.' Thirteen long years, all of them, every long day of all thirteen, in the steadfast love of God.

What has God been doing? Can we discover from the story what has been in God's mind, as He has been

seemingly heartless and relentless in His treatment of
the young man?

When I was younger, I used to think that this was
the really simple question. Of course we can see what
God is doing, I would think. God is working it so that
Joseph will be Prime Minister of Egypt on about
£20,000 a year plus a three-storey villa and all the
etceteras (and don't forget the *Cadillac*!). What a
simple question, I would say. Just have a look at Joseph
now that he is really into his stride. What a man!
Watch him at work. Seven years of plenty, and he has
certainly been throwing his weight about. Every store-
house in every city is stacked to the rafters with food
and grain. He has so much stuff stored up that he has
lost track of it all. But it's all there, and it's still pouring in. Bounty immeasurable.

And he himself has two sons. What are their names,
Joseph?

'The elder is called Manasseh.'

Why Manasseh? What does that name mean?

'It means "Making to forget".'

Forget? Forget what?

'All the hardship. And' (wistfully he says this) 'all
my father's house; my own family.'

And the younger?

'His name is Ephraim. That means "To be fruitful",
for God has made me fruitful in the land of my afflic-
tion.'

Yes, there has been a lot of balm poured on the
wounds, but these are wounds that can never heal.
What a blessing to be so busy, then, as he tries to
forget. For the years of famine are now there, and
Joseph is properly tangled up in his job.

Everybody's food ran out. So they went to Joseph.
He sold the stored grain, and collected all their cash.
When they had no more money, they were still short
of food, and back again to Joseph they came, this time
begging not to be allowed to starve. 'Sure,' said Joseph.
'You can have as much grain as you need. But not for
nothing. I'll exchange the grain for your livestock if

you haven't any money.' Joseph collected all the herds
and flocks and horses and donkeys!

Next year they were still in trouble. No money, no
stock. But still hungry. That was no trouble to Joseph.
He just took over the title deeds of all their proper-
ties! And then the next time signed them all up as
slaves! Only the priests were exempted, because they
had nationalized religion, and the priests all drew their
salaries from Pharaoh, and of course could still buy
food.

Then it was that the real genius of Joseph showed
out. It is one thing to own all the money and the
animals and the land *and* the people. But if you own
all the people as slaves you have to feed them and look
after them. And Joseph was far too shrewd to do that.
He has the instincts of a Capitalist, not a left-wing
Socialist.

'Listen,' he said to them, 'I have today bought you
and your land for Pharaoh. But what I'll do is give you
seed. Then you go and sow the seed and work your
farms, but twenty per cent of all the crops go to
Pharaoh. He owns the land, and you too, but you can
keep four-fifths of the produce, and he'll be satisfied
with one-fifth.'

And as I read this, and chuckle at the shrewd head
on young Joseph, who is now doing so famously for
his master Pharaoh, something begins to make ticking
noises in my small brain. I want to stop and think.

Is this the goal God had in mind, in all those thirteen years of misery? All this cash and cattle and what-
not just being stacked away in Pharaoh's vaults? Oh,
I know, a decent fat salary for Joseph, and riding
round in the *Cadillac*, and all that. But is that all God
had in mind in those terrible years in the stinking
dungeons? (Can I ever forget the butler—the graceless
cur who just forgot Joseph, and left him there to rot
for two more awful years?) If that should be the game
God is playing, then either He's playing it very very
poorly; or else it's a very very poor game.

And Joseph is not the only player, remember. I can

think of many who were equally in the strong steadfast love of God, and as He Himself tells us, some of them 'suffered mocking and scourging, and even chains and imprisonment. They were stoned, they were sawn in two, they were killed with the sword; they went about in skins of sheep and goats, destitute, afflicted, ill-treated—of whom the world was not worthy—wandering over deserts and mountains, and in dens and caves of the earth.'

No. A thousand times no! This is not the truth of the story at all. This is not what God is aiming at. God is not a Materialist, not a Merchant, thinking of dubloons and ducats and dollars. God is love. And He is doing something for Joseph, something *in* Joseph, that all the money and all the power and all the greatness of all the Pharaohs—and all the other kings on earth—couldn't start to do for Joseph. God is working out in Joseph something that only heaven can achieve. Can we find this?

I think we can. But we have to come to the very end of the story as it is recorded in the book of Genesis before the truth shows clearly. There have been many chapters in between—chapters filled with the fascinating account of how Joseph met up with his brothers. Of how the ten who had so gladly diced him and sold him into slavery came down to Egypt to buy food in the great famine. It tells of how they didn't recognize him; but he couldn't possibly miss them, of course.

And as he recognized them, bowing themselves to the ground, seeking to buy food from him, flashing into his memory was the thought of the dreams he had told them, away back as a seventeen-year-old. Those fateful dreams. We see the tremendous emotional conflict going on in Joseph, as he faced his ten half-brothers; and longed to meet his full-brother, young Benjamin.

Read, if you like—and you must be moved, as well as puzzled, if you read—of Simeon, the hostage; and the money in the sacks and Benjamin at last, and the cup in Benjamin's sack, and the hot tears of the final reunion. And of Judah, smooth-tongued Judah, telling glib half-lies to his father. Then Jacob, tottering old white-headed Jacob, is there, and Pharaoh is blessed by old Jacob, and they all settle down in Goshen, good grazing land near the Nile delta.

There also you will read how old Jacob died. But before he died he did what he had always intended to do. He passed on the patriarchal blessing to Joseph's two sons. To him Joseph had always been the eldest son, and now Joseph's sons receive the blessing.

Just watch him giving the blessing. Look! Can it be true?

Yes, it is true enough. One hundred and forty-seven years of age, the old man is, yet still showing the deep twisting conflict that had so warped and distorted him from his birth. For as the poor old fellow took the two grandsons to give them the blessing, it was on the head of Ephraim, the younger, that it rested his right hand. It just couldn't be for him to give the firstborn the rights that for himself, the second twin, had such tragic and poignant significance.

So Jacob died, still twisted, still complex, still showing the scars of the emotional insecurities that had so profoundly affected that whole page of human history.

Then Pharaoh turned up trumps, and provided transport and a whole army escort, with all the trimmings, to take old Jacob's embalmed body back to Canaan for burial. All the twelve brothers, together with their families, made the trip. So the old patriarch was buried alongside his father Isaac and his grandfather Abraham.

After he had buried his father, Joseph came back to Egypt with his brothers and the rest of the party who had gone up to Canaan with him. And then, at this point of the narrative, when you would think the whole thing is finished telling, only twelve verses left in the whole of the book of Genesis, the great truth is made clear. Clear in one of those sparkling little pieces of narrative in which Bible writing abounds, flashing out a truth of heavenly magnitude; yet told as it were so casually that the rebel, the man who is up against

God and the things which God does, would never see it there at all.

It is told in a tiny incident concerning the ten elder brothers. They put their heads together in secret and serious conference. We must imagine the details of this conference, because only the end result is recorded. But it's not hard to imagine it. Let's pretend we're listening.

'Listen. Do any of you seriously think Joseph has got over what we did to him?'

'Not a bit of it. He's no fool. He had a pretty sticky time for a good many years. I'll bet he's stewing away over it all day.'

'Yes. And you remember those sickening dreams he had as a youngster? You can take your oath he hasn't forgotten them. And remember how he told us he only got his present job because of a dream. It's too risky altogether for my liking. Any old tick of the clock someone's going to turn up with a dream that will set him going, and it'll be curtains for us.'

'Yes. But why hasn't he done anything to us before? We've been here seventeen years now. Do you think he may have forgotten all about what we did to him?'

'Oh yeah! How silly can you get? He never forgets anything. Watch how he runs this country. He's got the memory of an elephant! I'll tell you why he has left us alone. It's because of the old man. You know how our Dad used to skite about having had twelve sons, even if he spoke of Rachel as his only wife. And Joseph just hasn't wanted to upset the old man, they were so close to each other. But now Father Jacob's dead, I don't like our chances, and I reckon we had better cook something up, or we'll all be dead ducks.'

'My oath!' This from Simeon, I can well imagine. 'I'm all for playing safe. You remember how he picked on me and kept me as a hostage when we first came down to Egypt? Remember? He bound me up in front of you all. And don't forget he knew all the time who we were, and which one I was. I've always hated his guts, the young rat, and I'll never believe he has just

forgotten. No, sir! I don't like the idea of being bound
up again, not one little bit.'

'Say. . . . That gives me an idea.' (We are not told
who said this first, but I'd guess it was Judah—he is
the expert at cooking up a likely-looking line of plaus-
ible half-truth.) 'Yes. . . . Quite an idea. What say we
tell him—ever so meek, you know, and plenty of
"Your humble servants, My Lord"—tell him that
before he died our father asked us to take a special
dying request to Joseph, saying it was his particular
hope that Joseph would forgive us for all our nasty
little tricks. You get the idea? Play it up as coming
from Father Jacob, and lay on the jam and eat humble
pie, and I reckon it will work.'

'So do I. That's a brilliant idea, Judah.' 'I'm with
you too.' 'It's a jolly good scheme, and . . .' '. . . we've
got to find something.'

And so it was agreed. The time and occasion were
picked and planned, and Joseph was given the phoney
message.

And then, in one sentence, in six monosyllables, the
secret is out. All the wonder of the purpose of God in
the seemingly terrible hammering He has been giving
to Joseph, is now shown to us.

We read that when the message was given to Joseph
he 'wept when they spoke to him'. Yes, in that cryptic
statement is found the amazing answer to this thirty
years of God's working. If you can understand Joseph
weeping when he heard this so obviously cooked-up
yarn, then you are on the way to understanding all
the wonder of the 'steadfast love of God' working in
the life of Joseph or of any other saint.

Joseph wept because he was so upset to see his
brothers so fearful, when they had no need to be afraid.
He realized, in the lightning-fast way his mind worked,
that he had caused them years of fear and uncertainty,
and all because they had so completely mistaken him.
His gracious manner and generous attitude wasn't a
front, a mask, at all. He wasn't masquerading behind
a façade of magnanimity, satisfying and building up

his ego, as he made his brothers literally eat out of his hand.

No, all that is gone, gone entirely. Not veneered over by some further pride and conceit, but rooted right out for ever. That is what God has been doing. No wonder He has not been limited by emotion and comfort. This is that breath-taking wonder of 'new-birth', 're-creation', 'being made perfect', of which the New Testament tells so constantly.

Yes. Here we have been reading the life of a man who lived nearly four thousand years ago, and learning from this case-history the wonder of what God does to His people, as He cares for them in His steadfast love.

We have seen God take one of His men, this time a young man, an insufferable, intolerable, conceited spoilt brat of a prig of a young man, and in steadfast love turn this seemingly hopeless case into a genuinely humble, gracious fifty-year-old.

Of course Joseph wept. Not weeping for self-pity, that his brothers should think so ill of him; but weeping because of his concern for their concern. It filled him with sadness to think of the distress they had been through, as with his quick mind he realized that in all of those years they had been in fear and doubt because of him. Their fears were so groundless. He just wasn't like that at all. 'Joseph wept when they spoke to him.'

Did Joseph know what happened to himself, in himself? I don't for a moment think so. Do you think Moses ever recognized that it was meekness that God was creating in him? Could he possibly see that in him God was taking the one who was unquestionably the strongest, greatest, most impressive giant of a man in all history, and perfecting in him meekness 'more than all men that were on the face of the earth'?

And as with Moses, where all the other greatnesses were not sacrificed for meekness, but rather strengthened by the new God-given grace, so with Joseph. His extraordinary dependability, his sexual chastity, his mental alertness—all these great personal gifts which undoubtedly made his priggish conceit so much more intolerable, were not supplanted by humility, but were now vastly enhanced by it.

This is always the way with God. He knows His Joseph completely and in detail. He recognizes in His young servant the quality of reliability which has been passed on from Abraham, perhaps; the resourcefulness of Jacob; maybe the capacity for imagination (Alexander Whyte says of imagination: 'There is nothing so noble in all that is within us'), which may well have been his heritage from Isaac, insecure, introspective Isaac. Yes, God sees all these great and good qualities which also came from Himself into the lives of Joseph's forefathers, and so to the young man of dreams; but God also sees in stark and naked truth the arrogance and pride which were with them. And because God is love, because He wills His best for Joseph, He has been at work in him, up-rooting the thing that is unworthy, and creating instead the thing that is good.

Is that the end of Joseph's story, you ask? Yes. That is the end of any saint's story. Joseph lived on for many more years on this earth, but that is the end of his story. The later years are like those earlier thirty. The same thing happening, as he remains in the steadfast love of God. That is why I said before that this story is really like all the stories in the Bible. This is what is always happening to men of God.

At some stage in the process (and God Himself alone says when) the scene moves from this material world where it all began, to that heavenly world where it is all to be completed. God has not told anything of how or by what process, in the ages to come, He will complete this new life; but He has assured us that it is all of surpassing joy and delight.

The case-history of Joseph is there for us to learn from, to help us understand what the Master means when He tells us that 'we all . . . are being changed into his likeness from one degree of glory to another'. It illustrates in some small but clear human experience what He means when He tells us that 'He will re-make these wretched bodies of ours to resemble his own glorious body, by that power of his which makes him the master of everything that is'. This is the story which should surely strengthen us in our will to follow 'him who is able to keep us from falling and to present us before his glory without fault and with unspeakable joy'.

What a programme! What a wonder! One day we will see clearly what is as yet only a distorted mirror-image—for He will show 'for all time the tremendous generosity of the grace and kindness he has expressed towards us in Christ Jesus'—we will see how He has 'lifted us right out of the old life to take our place with him in Christ in the Heavens'.

'The Lord was with Joseph and showed him steadfast love.'